SELECTIONS FROM

Portals to the Past

CLAIRE MASTERS

Claire Masters

MᶜM

TABLE OF CONTENTS

FASHION

PERSONALITIES

This publication was made possible
by contributions from:

John & Linda Baker

The James Barcus Family
in memory of Nancy Bidwell Barcus

Agnes Warren Barnes

Margaret Boyce Brown
in memory of Shepherd Spencer Neville Brown, Sr.

Joe & Billie Brownfield

The Fentress Foundation

Jim & Nell Hawkins

Ann & Roane Lacy, Jr.

Claude & Becky Lindsey

Mary Myers Mann

Norma Sheehy Rhodes

Thank you.

PREFACE: THE HISTORIC PERSPECTIVE

I've always had a curiosity about the historic aspect of a thing. Sitting in the dentist's chair, I begin to wonder about dental care in the far past, before tooth-paste and the electric drill. When I enter a shoe repair shop, I think of the little slipper, now preserved in a Paris museum, that once fell from Queen Marie Antoi-nette's foot as she ascended the scaffold. When I spot a tall crane dominating a building site, I remember that the crane was invented by Philippo Brunelleschi during the Italian Renaissance so that he could erect his monumental Duomo in Florence, the building that marked the end of the medieval period.

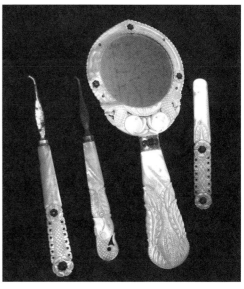

Mother-of-pearl dental instruments which belonged to Dr. Alexander Archer Beville— one of Waco's earliest dentists. Current owner is Dr. T. Bradford Willis.

Years ago, when I lived in the San Francisco Bay Area, I began taking courses at a nearby community college. The very first subject that I discovered in the Diablo Valley College catalog was Fashion History. That thought-provoking study of fashion history changed and enriched my life far more than I could have ever dreamed. I can see now that, ideally, everyone should develop some sort of passion, an all-abiding interest in a subject that will dominate one's thoughts and actions throughout a lifetime.

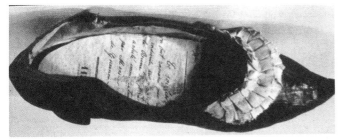

Marie Antoinette's shoe

From that single course in fashion history, I have spun off many projects: collected vintage garments and accessories; written, spoken, and traveled with fashion/textiles in mind; curated and created 28 exhibits from an historic collection and have compiled a credible personal library on the subject. The instructor of that fashion history course, Hal Madsen, who was head of the two-year program in fashion design, became a dear friend and mentor.

When I asked to borrow some of his fashion history slides to copy, he said, "Yes, you may, but if anything should happen to my precious teaching slides, you and I will jump off the Golden Gate Bridge together."

Using Hal Madsen's slides as the nucleus of my collection, I began to amass dozens of fashion history slides. From these, I gave programs on the subject to Bay Area women's organizations, tailoring my presentations to each group's needs. I also began to present a fashion show that highlighted my personal hat collection. This proved to be an inspired idea; and by the time I moved back to Waco with the hats, I had refined my show to a "T."

My husband and I retired here almost 28 years ago. Re-introduction to my hometown took the form of one of my hat fashion shows. The Waco Garden Center had need of a fundraiser program and I offered my services. I remember that Lois Elliott was president of the Garden Clubs then. I used their members for models, putting them all in simple black dresses. I provided the commentary as well as the hats with period-appropriate accessories, such as furs, handbags, gloves, and jewelry. I remember the audience reaction to all my marvelous old hats from the first half of the 20th century. The ladies had never seen anything like it.

Afterward, as people drifted up to say hello, I was introduced to a small, silver-haired lady, Bobbie Barnes. She cried out, "Where have you been? I have been looking for you!" She told me about the large group of Victorian and early 20th century garments that she had stored in her basement. Bobbie sensed that with my fashion history background, I might be able to help her with the collection that she had been storing for Historic Waco Foundation. So that's how I began to look after all the garments and flat textiles that I would ultimately title, the Heritage Collection.

This was just about the time that HWF began its efforts to accession each and every item in all four of our house museums, from every carpet to every teacup. It would prove to be a daunting task, spanning several years and employing dozens of volunteers. Swept up in the effort, I began to catalog more than 3,000 garments and flat textiles from Bobbie Barnes' basement. If I had been told that it would take twenty years to accession them, I wonder if I would have initiated the attempt. Of course, along the way, I learned so much about the museum world and expanded my knowledge of the subject.

For example, whenever I began the task of accessioning a Victorian dress, I could spend an entire day measuring and describing each part of the complex garment. There might have been half a dozen separate pieces to the single outfit: skirt, petticoats, bodice, peplum, cuffs, and collar. I learned the importance of working slowly and steadily in order to leave a perfectly intact paper trail to each item.

Working with such artifacts has honed my descriptive powers considerably.

For the first time, Historic Waco Foundation began to tap the resources of Baylor University's Museum Studies program. A brilliant student named Irit Lev was hired as an intern. Her job was to instruct me, as well as all the other volunteers, in the correct procedures of cataloging and proper storage.

I joined Costume Society of America, whose membership is made up of professionals in the museum world. CSA produces an annual fashion symposium, which I began to attend at my own cost, traveling to Colonial Williamsburg, Montreal, Canada, San Antonio, Dallas, Santa Fe, New York City, Houston, and Atlanta. I was even invited to deliver a paper at the CSA Salt Lake City symposium. Rubbing elbows with the elite of museum curators was a heady experience and I made many valuable contacts there, always surprised that I was accepted as a peer.

Travel was another way to improve my background in fashion history and the care and exhibition of old garments. In our younger days, my husband and I were avid travelers to Spain, England, France, Italy, as well as many destinations throughout the U.S.A. I always made a point of writing ahead to the curators of particular museums that had noteworthy clothing collections. Might I be granted a courtesy tour of their storage and exhibit facilities? I always introduced myself as a volunteer, self-trained curator of a modest collection in Central Texas. I was amazed at the generosity of such curators. No one has ever denied my request.

My biggest coup was the Musée de la Mode of the Louvre in Paris. As usual, I had written ahead and upon my arrival, I phoned for an appointment. Certainly, the assistant curator would welcome me to the Louvre's special wing that is devoted to fashion and the decorative arts.

One thing about the French, they seem to have a special fascination with Texas, that mythic land of cowboys and Indians. There's a certain mystique about John Wayne country, and I'm always aware of its impact when I introduce myself to foreigners as a Texan. Generally speaking, Europeans know New York, California, and Texas. Heaven help you if you're from Nebraska or one of those "square" states. I have heard that certain riding groups in France participate in reenactments of cowboy and Indian battles. So perhaps that is why the gates to one of the greatest collections were opened to me. If I had turned up wearing a ten-gallon hat and cowboy boots, I don't think those Frenchies would have been surprised.

Madame gave me an entire morning, explaining the various new exhibits being developed. She invited me to inspect a new acquisition, a gown designed by Charles Frederick Worth, the 19th century's most sought-after Parisian designer. She took me upstairs to view an enormous room under the eaves of that ancient building, where conservators worked on precious garments from the collection. I came away with so much information, as well as a sense that my work back in Waco was vindicated.

On my return, I began to see the possibility of creating exhibits from our own invaluable historic resource. Originally entrusted to Bobbie Barnes, many of the garments and flat textiles are from Waco and central Texas families. Over the last twenty years, I have created 28 exhibits, ranging from military, maternity, accessories of all sorts, swimwear to children's clothing.

INTRODUCTION

by Bruce Kabat, Assistant Managing Editor, Waco Tribune-Herald

In 2000, I made a "cold call" to ask a favor of someone I never had met. The lasting result has been a warm professional relationship that brightens many a workday for me.

It was in late September, several days after the passing of 93-year-old Lavonia Jenkins Barnes, co-founder of Historic Waco Foundation. At the time, I was editor of *Waco Today* magazine, a monthly publication of the Waco Tribune-Herald. Although I was up against a deadline for the next issue, I wanted to pay tribute to the woman who had a profound impact on the preservation of Waco's heritage.

Who better to write a remembrance of Bobbie Barnes than her protégée, Claire Masters? I knew of Claire from her involvement in various HWF projects that we had covered in the magazine. I also had heard her described as "formidable," an intriguing word that ranges in definition from "causing fear and apprehension" to "inspiring awe and wonder."

We spoke on the phone, and Claire graciously accepted the assignment. I cleared off the back two pages of the magazine and hoped that my "untested" writer would do justice to the subject.

Had I known Claire then as I do now, I wouldn't have worried. The very next day, she brought me a sensitively written, 750-word piece in which she shared some fond memories of her friend and mentor. Achieving the proper tone in such a tribute can be a challenge, but Claire handled it expertly—seasoned by her experience in writing for newspapers on the West Coast years ago. During a time of personal loss and mourning, it had to be a difficult task for her.

Soon thereafter, we launched her column for *Waco Today* called 'Portals to the Past', focusing on Historic Waco Foundation's house museums and the treasures they contain.

Claire also has written many travel pieces, transporting readers to the Tate Gallery in London, the ruins of Pompeii, Italy and Mont-Saint-Michel in France. Each story is enriched by her sharp eye for detail and vast knowledge of history, architecture, decorative arts, cuisine...well, let's just say the list goes on.

As much as I value her contributions to the magazine, I count it an even greater blessing to have made her acquaintance. She always stops by to chat when she turns in a story or photos for her column, even though I've moved on to other duties at the newspaper. I have found her "formidable" indeed, but only in the most awe-inspiring sense.

She loves a good story and exudes an infectious glee when tackling an assignment. Our conversations might hopscotch from Edwardian fashions to 17th century Dutch artists to the use of exclamation points (she knows I eschew them, but she still found a way to slip them into her stories.)

And now she has compiled some of her columns into this volume titled "Selections from Portals to the Past." Proceeds from sales of the book, naturally, will benefit Historic Waco Foundation.

I don't use exclamation points for just anyone, Claire, but here's wishing you great success!

PROLOGUE

People always ask me where I find my story ideas. My answer is the same today as it was forty years ago when I first began writing freelance for San Francisco Bay Area newspapers.

Knock on any door and you'll find a story or perhaps more than one story. Turn over a pebble and discover an entire microscopic world of plant and animal life to write about. Story ideas are easy to initiate, but researching and writing them can be challenging.

It was during the year 2000 when I heard that the editor of *Waco Today* was looking for someone to write a new column, which would be totally devoted to Historic Waco Foundation. I immediately volunteered to go down to the *Waco Tribune-Herald* and speak to editor Bruce Kabat. Would I have enough material to write a monthly column about one organization, year after year? Having a familiarity with our organization and its holdings, I assured him that Historic Waco Foundation would be an endless source of inspiration.

Can you imagine? Here in Waco, our local newspaper runs a monthly column totally devoted to our Historic Waco Foundation. We are probably the only organization in the entire country that has an outlet to publicize its historic house museums, their contents, special events, and exhibits. This book can be categorized as cultural/social history, describing how people lived in past times.

Here, I have collected some of my most popular Portals to the Past columns. Generally, they concentrate on architecture, the decorative arts, personalities , textiles, and fashion history. I particularly had fun with a tiny button from the HWF textile collection. Of course, it wasn't just any old button. Across its surface was the word "Interurban." This button must have been from the uniform of an Interurban train conductor. The Interurban consisted of several street cars joined together, which ran quite efficiently between Waco and Dallas in the first half of the 20th century.

Occasionally, my column would be about an individual, such as Jacob de Cordova. In the early days of Texas, Waco attracted men such as de Cordova like a magnet. He was personable, well educated, spoke several languages as well as some Indian dialects, and he had an instinct for land development. It was he, along with George Erath, who laid out the City of Waco and sold property to newcomers. The growing community was fortunate that de Cordova generously donated land for public schools, hospitals, and various religious denominations. His picture hangs in McCulloch House Museum today.

Most importantly, Historic Waco Foundation's four house museums have provided inspiration for the bulk of my Portals to the Past columns. These restored Victorian landmarks, all built just after the Civil War, are absolutely stuffed with fine furniture, art, and family mementoes. They have provided a never-ending range of stories about all their furnishings and the families who built and lived in them.

It has been a delight to have been blessed with Portals to the Past. Researching each column, I learned more and more about Historic Waco Foundation, my hometown of Waco, and the State of Texas. I have received many kind notes from my readers, which were always welcome. I hope to hear from readers of this book, as well.

I would like to thank Carlos Sanchez, former editor of the *Waco Tribune-Herald* for granting permission to reprint my work in this book. All profits will go toward various projects of Historic Waco Foundation. Editor Bruce Kabat and subsequent editors have all been generous with their encouragement over the decade of this column's existence. Portals to the Past column has been my portal to the heart of Historic Waco Foundation and all its riches.

In writing my columns, I have tried to put a human face on each story with all the day-to-day working and living that these Wacoans experienced. Though the stories in this book relate to Waco, Texas and its particular history, the reader will quickly discern that there is a certain universal appeal here. All of these historic houses, their furnishings, and their inhabitants could just as well have occurred in any other city—large or small—of this country.

This book is dedicated to the memory of Mrs. Maurice (Bobbie) Barnes, who was in part responsible for rescuing and restoring our four Historic Waco Foundation houses. With herculean zeal and energy, this little Dresden teacup of a woman fought the good fight to secure as much of Waco's architectural past as she possibly could.

Bobbie was my mentor and I, her faithful follower. At her death, she bequeathed to me her library of several hundred books on the decorative arts, landscape architecture, history, art history, and biography. I like to think that she would have been pleased with this collection of my Portals to the Past.

The Author

ARCHITECTURE

BLESS THE LADIES OF OUR LAND

In 1966, a group of Dallas women stood on the front porch of the city's only remaining substantial antebellum building—Millermore. Bravely, they defied the bulldozers sent to raze the lovely old place. Evidently, the land was destined to become a parking lot. At the last minute, a constable arrived with the restraining order that the ladies had previously requested. Millermore was saved!

That determined little group of women went on to found the Dallas County Heritage Society. They saw to it that Millermore and the nearby Miller family log cabin and playhouse were dismantled and moved from Oak Cliff across the Trinity River and reconstructed on the present site. These buildings formed the nucleus of Dallas Old City Park, now known as Dallas Heritage Village, which became the city's first official bicentennial project, ten years before that celebratory year.

Time and time again, I have seen the efforts of such forward-looking citizens as the heroines of the Dallas County Heritage Society. What would our country have done without their dogged efforts and foresight? Why is it so often the ladies who have to raise money and brave the bulldozers in order to save fragments of our precious history?

I lived in San Francisco in the 1960s when people were just beginning to be aware of the importance of conserving architectural relics of the past. The approaching bicentennial must have had some influence there, but the muddle-headed San Francisco city fathers decided that the cable cars would have to be removed and the rails torn up. Millions of dollars were required for renovations. Somehow, they just couldn't see that a 19th century cable car system was practical.

One little old lady named Mrs. Klussmann thought otherwise. What does practicality have to do with the colorful, historic little cars? She attended every public meeting on the subject, flailing her cane around and making a general nuisance of herself. Each time, she would be dragged out, kicking and screaming. Naturally, the newspaper photographers had a field day. Her efforts may have been undignified, but brave Mrs. Klussmann helped to save one of the most important symbols of San Francisco. Mayor Diane Feinstein also supported the rebuilding of the cable car system and helped obtain federal funds to do so. Today, because of the vision and courage of these two women, the restored cable cars tootle up and down the hills of San Francisco, chug-full of tourists who happily pay big bucks for a ride to the stars.

Another result of the approaching bicentennial was the refurbishing of the White House, the traditional home of the United States President. During the early 1960s, First Lady Jackie Kennedy—a woman of consummate taste and judgment— decided that the public rooms of the White House had been neglected for  far too long. The unofficial custom of retiring Presidents' leaving with their choice of furnishings had stripped the place of much of its historic furniture. Even the widowed Mrs. Lincoln had been guilty of this act. So, Mrs. Kennedy formed The Committee for the Preservation of the White House, a board of decorative and fine art experts who began to research the subject and to search for surviving pieces. Owners were contacted and asked to give (or sell) them back for exhibition in the White House.

One of the most powerful words in the English language is "ask." Amazingly, many American citizens came forward to cooperate with Mrs. Kennedy and her board. Everyone remembers watching the television program of Mrs. Kennedy as she introduced the American public to all the new historic acquisitions. Jackie is gone from the scene now, but her board still functions as an official watchdog of White House interiors.

In 1905, a Texas woman named Clara Driscoll paid the back taxes on a shabby old San Antonio building. Today, it's incomprehensible that no one else thought it appropriate to save the iconic building that epitomizes the Texas Revolution. The State of Texas turned it over to the Daughters of the Republic of Texas, organized in 1898. The ladies now efficiently operate the Alamo as an entrance-free museum at no cost to the citizens of Texas.

Just before the Civil War, a woman from the Carolinas, Ann Pamela Cunningham, formed the Mount Vernon Ladies' Association. The home of our first president had stood, empty and deteriorating since the turn of the century when Martha Washington died. Miss Cunningham convinced the great-nephew of George Washington to sell it to her organization, in the hopes that the women of America would send in their dollar donations to pay for Mount Vernon.

2

Successful in this endeavor, the lady then confronted the leaders of each side of the brewing conflict—Abraham Lincoln and Jefferson Davis—requesting that all Mount Vernon properties be considered off-limits to either army, Union or Confederate.

All through that devastating war, battles raged around Mount Vernon, but the property remained inviolate during that conflict. Miss Cunningham's efforts saved Mount Vernon from further deterioration and the depredations of war. Today, George Washington's beautifully restored home is owned and operated as a house museum by the Mount Vernon Ladies' Association, not the U.S. government or the state of Virginia.

Here in Waco, we were blessed with our own intrepid preservationist, Mrs. Maurice (Bobbie) Barnes. As one of the founders of Historic Waco Foundation (HWF), Bobbie was active in helping to save six Waco landmark homes. They are: East Terrace, Earle-Napier-Kinnard, Fort House, and McCulloch, which are operated by HWF as house museums, as well as Hoffmann House, which serves as its office.

Bobbie and a Waco woman friend, Nell Pape, also rescued, moved, restored, and furnished the antebellum Earle Harrison home on Fifth Street, which was facing wrecking crews because of its original location near Highway 35. It is operated independently today.

COLUMNS AND CAPITALS OF WACO
Reading Waco's Architecture

About fifteen years ago, I was invited to give Historic Waco Foundation's annual spring lecture. I chose to analyze elements of Waco's architecture as they relate to the past. This article also appeared in *Waco Heritage & History* magazine, Fall, 2007.

If you are a student of classical architecture, you needn't travel to Greece or Rome to study its different forms. Waco is an absolute hotbed of classical references. All you need is a bit of knowledge to recognize the many historical architectural references that surround us in our city.

Some years ago, I was chatting with Professor John Alexander from the School of Architecture of Texas A&M. He had come to Waco to give the Barnes Decorative Arts lecture on the history of architecture. Afterward, I drove him around Waco to show off some of our own architecture. He was enchanted, declaring that, "Waco is a gem because it's a backwater in the most positive sense. Waco has retained much of its architectural heritage while so many other cities have destroyed theirs."

As Professor Alexander explained that day, architecture is the expression of the character and perceptions of a people. Architecture is determined by all conditions around it: terrain, climate, available materials, politics, religion, technology, and the general level of wealth and culture achieved by the people who live, play, work, or worship in its buildings.

There is evidence of our architectural roots all around us here in the middle of Texas: the antiquity of Egyptian, Greek, and Roman styles. We are also blessed with buildings that draw inspiration from later times, such as Byzantine, Romanesque, Gothic, Renaissance, and 17th century Baroque.

EGYPTIAN

Some of the world's oldest surviving architecture can be found in Egypt. Many surviving edifices date as far back as 5000 BC, perhaps even older. The legions of Alexander the Great, 332 BC, and later, Julius Caesar, 50 BC, made their mark in Egypt. Otherwise, Egypt's sleeping past remained hidden from Western Europe for thousands of years. Learned people knew about the fabled land across the Mediterranean, but few had actually traveled to that mysterious place.

Napoléon Bonaparte's invasion in 1798 finally introduced Egypt to the modern world. The Rosetta Stone was discovered at that time and taken back to France, where a brilliant young fellow named Jean-Francois Champollion decoded those enigmatic Egyptian hieroglyphics, thereby revealing an entire world of study for historians and scholars.

For their temples and palaces, the Egyptians preferred a geometric, formal layout. With all that sand available, the basic building material was unbaked brick that had to be assembled with a greater thickness at the base and lower wall. This accounts for the slightly raked walls that tilt inward. Even though the buildings were monumental and coldly structural, the Egyptians lavished color on interior and exterior surfaces to depict the world around them. Stylized motifs of the lotus, lily, papyrus, reed, date palm, the lion, ibis, bull, sphinx, snake, eagle, dog, cat, and horse are easily recognized on walls and columns.

A good example of ancient Egyptian architecture is the exquisite Temple of Isis that once stood on Philae Island. Open to the hot Egyptian sun, its massive columns were covered with colorful designs and their capitals imitated the palm. Unfortunately, much of it fell victim to the waters of the Aswan Dam that inundated the area in the 1960s.

Grand Lodge of Texas Museum & Library • Waco, Texas

Compare Egypt's architecture with the 1940s Masonic Grand Lodge on Columbus Avenue. Dallas architects Broad and Nelson referred back to Egypt of the Old Testament for this severely formal and geometric building. It is meant to be a replica of the Temple of Solomon in Jerusalem as described in the Old Testament. Carved on its front is the story of Solomon's temple being built, with the cedars of

5

Lebanon being cut down and the stone being quarried. Tradition tells us that Moses himself directed the building of the great Temple. The charismatic leader of the Hebrews had been brought up in the Egyptian court and most likely would have been influenced by its architecture.

Lee Lockwood Library & Museum • Waco, Texas

Another Egyptian-style building that we drive by every day is the Lee Lockwood Library & Museum on West Waco Drive. Though it was built thousands of years after Egypt's heyday, an Egyptian Pharaoh would nevertheless feel quite at home today if he were to enter the gates of the Lee Lockwood Library fronted by stylized sphinxes.

GREEK

Across the Mediterranean, we find our next important source of architectural inspiration. There on the Greek islands and mainland, some of the most sublime examples of building design can be found. Erected in the 5th century BC under the direction of Pericles during the Golden Age of Greek civilization, the Parthenon in Athens is acknowledged as the quintessential masterpiece of all Greek architecture.

The ancient Greeks have given us more architectural design and motifs than any other source. Every first-year art history student learns about the Greek key design (imitating waves), egg and dart (symbolizing life and death) and the anthemion (a stylized honeysuckle blossom). These enduring designs and many others can be spotted all around our city, carved into building fronts, interiors, and furniture, as well.

Most important are the Greek classical orders that originally embellished their temples, such as the Parthenon. Its exterior is surrounded by Doric columns, the

oldest and most formal classical order. Ionic columns can be found in the interior of the great temple dedicated to Athena. It's interesting to note that the Greeks used no mortar. Building stones were hand-cut with mathematical precision using the most rudimentary instruments.

Parthenon • Athens, Greece

The Doric capital is quite plain with no embellishments. The columns of older Doric buildings are usually more massive than later ones. This order was altered by 16th century Italians and is known as Tuscan.

A good local example of the Doric is the Red Men Museum & Library on Speight Avenue, a dead ringer for Thomas Jefferson's Monticello which, in turn, was inspired by the 16th Italian architect Andrea Palladio, whose work was so deeply influenced by antiquity.

But remember, the columns and capitals on our modern buildings are usually made of wood, while the Greeks carved from marble. The Greek monuments, which have survived more than two thousand years of war, earthquakes, and vandalism will survive long after our wood and brick buildings have decayed.

Red Men Museum & Library • Waco, Texas

The next classical order is Ionic, which consists of two scroll-shaped volutes with anthemion and palmette shapes in-between. Over time, the Ionic has been interpreted in many ways. Ideally, its column is taller and more slender than the older Doric column. The Greeks used it for small buildings and interiors.

First Church of Christ Scientist
Waco, Texas

There are many examples of Waco buildings that incorporate the Ionic style: First Church of Christ Scientist on Columbus Avenue, the front of Waco High School and the little tempietto atop the Dr. Pepper Museum on Fifth Street. Over on Fourth and Webster, there are two handsome Ionic columns on the 19th century Greek revival Fort House Museum. Its front porch is topped with a gabled roof that might have been lifted from an ancient Greek temple.

Old Waco High School • Waco, Texas

(Above) Dr Pepper Museum Tempietto • Waco, Texas

(Left) Fort House Museum • Waco, Texas

8

Even though the building has been renovated and renamed, Chuck's Hilltop Shell gas station, most likely built in the 1930s at the top of Lakeshore Boulevard, was once fronted with Ionic columns and capitals. It must have been the only gas station in the country to be fronted with classical columns.

Chuck's Hilltop Shell station
Waco, Texas

Corinthian is the last of the Greek classical orders. It is decidedly the most decorative with a slender column and deeply carved capital. The design is taken from the frilly leaf of the acanthus plant that grows around the Mediterranean. As with the Ionic, the Corinthian can take many shapes. It was never very popular with the Greeks, but was enthusiastically adopted by the Romans who greatly admired and emulated Greek culture. With a heavy hand, the Romans would develop the Corinthian order for their own temples and palaces.

Corinthian order on the Temple of Vesta • Rome, Italy

9

The Corinthian order can be seen all over Waco. The portal on Columbus Avenue Baptist Church has a modified form of Corinthian. A handsome row of Corinthian columns marches across the front of the McLennan County Courthouse. In the interior of the Armstrong Browning Library at Baylor University, dedicated in 1951, are the most massive columns to be seen in Waco. They are unfluted, polished red Levanto marble with Corinthian capitals.

Columbus Avenue Baptist Church • Waco, Texas

McLean Foyer of Meditation, Armstrong Browning Library, Baylor University • Waco, Texas

McLennan County Courthouse • Waco, Texas

ROMAN

Pont du Gard • Nîmes, France

Much of Roman architecture is influenced by Greek design; however, the one thing that the Romans can definitely claim as their own is poured concrete. Yes, the concrete that our local contractors pour into roads and buildings is quite similar to the ancient Roman recipe. Evidence of Roman building techniques can be found all over Western Europe: aqueducts, bridges, and remnants of roads.

Rome's best-preserved antiquity is the 2nd century Pantheon. Even though its front gives the appearance of a classic Greek temple with Corinthian columns and capitals, its layout is basically an enormous drum with a 27-foot diameter round opening at the top called an *oculus*. Built

Pantheon • Rome, Italy

by Emperor Hadrianfor pagan rites, it was converted to a Christian church in the seventh century and is in amazingly perfect shape today.

That great soaring hemispherical dome is supported by poured concrete walls.

As with many other crafts, the technology of poured concrete was lost as the Roman civilization disintegrated and civilized life was lost to the Dark Ages. At that time, a dense fog of ignorance and anarchy descended over Western Europe.

With the collapse of the Roman Empire, Christianity became the standard-bearer of civilization. In order to survive the invasion of the Italian boot by the barbarian tribes from the north, the first Christian emperor, Constantine, moved his court to Byzantium in the Middle East in what is now Turkey. By then, a substantial population of Christians had developed there, and so he was welcomed to begin his city in AD 330.

BYZANTINE

Constantine named his new city *Constantinople*. The Roman architects who had followed him were naturally influenced by Middle Eastern design. Later, Emperor Justinian built Hagia Sophia (Church of Holy Wisdom) there in Constantinople. With its glowing Christian mosaics, Hagia Sophia set the style for all subsequent buildings in the Byzantine style.

Hagia Sophia • Istanbul, Turkey

Hagia Sophia is to Byzantine architecture what the Parthenon is to Greek architecture. Originally meant for Christian worship, it was transformed to a Muslim mosque after the Turks conquered Constantinople in 1453 and renamed

First Baptist Church • Waco, Texas

the city Istanbul. The Islamics covered all Hagia Sophia's Christian art with Arabic symbols and erected a slender minaret at each corner of the building.

A Waco building with faint echoes of the Byzantine style is First Baptist Church at Fifth and Webster whose cornerstone was laid in 1906. Its front is ringed with columns topped with capitals that have an Eastern flavor; its basic central dome is the Greek cross. Unlike many other churches in Waco, First Baptist lacks the conventional steeple or bell tower.

Another local church that has a touch of Eastern ornamentation is St. Johns United Methodist Church at the corner of 18th Street and Bosque

St. Johns United Methodist Church • Waco, Texas

Boulevard. Early Waco architects often mixed historic styles as seen in St. Johns. The façade is that of a Roman temple with exquisitely carved Roman capital letters above its columns, which are topped with capitals of an Oriental origin. (The apostrophe in St. Johns has been eliminated since they were never used in Roman lettering.)

ROMANESQUE

While Christianity flourished in the East, it barely survived in the West, retaining a toehold on the Adriatic coast of Italy. The flame of Christianity was kept alive by the establishment of monasteries by monks who settled in remote places such as Ireland. The 11th and 12th century style that evolved from the old Roman civilization was called Romanesque. St. Philibert Abbey in Tournus, France, in all its sublime simplicity, is a perfect example of the Romanesque. The barrel vault had been introduced; windows were small and lightly tinted. The stunning rose windows and soaring ceilings of the Gothic were yet to come.

The Dr Pepper Museum building on Fifth Street, designed by Milton Scott, has many architectural elements from Romanesque times: Italianate arches and rusticated stone work. Scott

Dr Pepper Museum • Waco, Texas

was an adherent of the well-known Henry Hobson Richardson who first introduced Romanesque to 19th century America.

GOTHIC

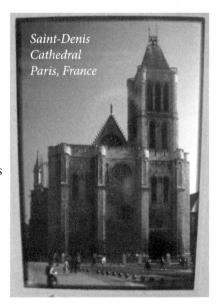

Saint-Denis Cathedral Paris, France

From the Romanesque was born the Gothic. This change coincided with the Roman Catholic Church's fascination with the Virgin Mary. Most of the Gothic cathedrals were built in her honor. However, there is one little church that straddles the Romanesque and the Gothic. It is considered the prototype of Gothic: Saint-Denis in Paris, built by a cleric named Suger in the 12th century. The low-pitched timber roof of the basilica type church was replaced by hand-hewn stone, which ensured safety as Suger's craftsmen built up and up toward heaven. He introduced the pointed arch windows and gave

Chartres Cathedral Rose Window • Chartres, France

us the beginnings of the rose window.

Those magnificent Gothic cathedrals, begun during the Age of Faith, can be found in such Western European countries as Spain, France, England, and Germany. Employing the barrel vault, steeples, buttresses, and stained glass windows, Gothic is spikily linear as though the builders were trying to reach God himself. An undeclared competition developed to build the highest cathedral; some buildings are known to have collapsed because of this urge to reach new heights.

Gothic cathedrals such as Chartres took hundreds of years to complete, one hand-hewn stone on top of another. The original builders never lived long enough to see their dream fulfilled. One generation of designers and craftsmen after another contributing their talents meant that a Gothic cathedral usually contains more than one style.

One idea that always puzzled me is that these builders employed hand-hewn stone, when all around Western Europe were examples of Roman ruins that had been made with concrete, as with the Pont du Gard in France. Why couldn't they have studied the makeup of the Roman ruins and then copied that successful technology for their cathedrals? Think of all the time and money that would have been saved. The answer is

*St. Louis Catholic Church Rose Window
Waco, Texas*

that those cathedrals were being built to honor the Virgin Mary. To use any idea from pagan Rome, no matter how practical, would have been unthinkable. Concrete

15

conjured up images of pagan alchemy, which could never have been allowed to tarnish the image of Notre Dame, our lady.

Driving around Waco, you see many Gothic references in our church steeples, windows, and portals. There are also several churches that have slight evidence of the Gothic which is decorative rather than structural. Compare Chartres' buttresses with Austin Avenue United Methodist Church in Waco, which was designed by the Dallas architectural firm of R.H.Hunt, 1923.

(Above) Buttresses on Reims Cathedral • Chartres, France

(Right) Stepped buttresses on Austin Avenue United Methodist Church • Waco, Texas

The sides of Austin Avenue United Methodist are ribbed with "stepped" buttresses, which have only a nominal supportive function. Chartres, on the other hand, really needed those exterior buttresses to support its tall, thin walls, made even more insubstantial by the many stained glass windows cut into them. By breaking up the monotony of those long brick walls, First Methodist's buttresses serve a decorative function.

ITALIAN RENAISSANCE

The Italians interpreted Gothic style in an entirely different manner. Climate was an important factor. In Northern Europe, the emphasis had been on height with large stained glass windows and a profusion of sculptural adornment. Farther south where the sun was stronger and the rain and snow less damaging, roofs were flatter and the horizontal line predominated. Because of the glare of the southern sun, windows were usually smaller.

St. Jerome Catholic Church • Waco, Texas

Italian Renaissance architecture is epitomized by Alberti's 15th century Santa Maria Novella in Florence, Italy. Its Tuscan Gothic style directly inspired by St. Jerome Catholic Church in west Waco, erected in the 1980s. The architectural firm was Raso Bailey Dudley & Rose of Waco. Closer examination of St. Jerome reveals that the exterior is finished in two shades of brick to resemble the various marbles used in Santa Maria Novella. Nevertheless, it's easy to recognize St. Jerome's Italian source of inspiration.

BAROQUE

For a perfect example of 17th century Baroque, consider our St. Francis on the Brazos Catholic Church, erected in 1931 by architect Roy E. Lane. St. Francis' origins can be traced to the 17th century baroque Cathedral of Santiago de Campostela in Spain.

St. Francis on the Brazos Catholic Church • Waco, Texas

TODAY

As you drive around our fair city, give a nod here and there to Waco's architectural riches. And the next time you attend a football game at Baylor's Floyd Casey stadium, consider its ancient antecedent, the Greek theater. The influences of western civilization's past are all around us in our own Texas architecture. They richly deserve to be acknowledged, treasured, and preserved.

Floyd Casey Stadium
Waco, Texas

EARLE-NAPIER-KINNARD HOUSE MUSEUM
814 South Fourth Street

As its name indicates, Earle-Napier-Kinnard House has been occupied by three families. The house began as a small two-room brick structure. These two rooms serve the house today as its kitchen. This original portion of Earle-Napier-Kinnard House was built by John Baylis Earle. Though the house was small, it most likely was surrounded by dependencies such as a kitchen, a smoke house, and a small barn. The exact date cannot be established since building permits were not required in those days.

John Baylis Earle, the son of a wealthy Mississippi doctor and plantation owner, moved to Waco in 1855. He was trained as a lawyer and though he died young, he was a man of achievement. He married Emma Cynthia Nelson in 1858 and moved his wife into his little home. They would have four children.

Mrs. Earle was the daughter of Allison Nelson who hailed from Georgia. Moving to Texas in 1856, Nelson served under Lawrence S. Ross as an Indian agent. At the outbreak of the Civil War, he was elected to the command of the Second Division of Holmes' Army in Arkansas. He fell ill of a fever and died in Arkansas in 1862.

Young Earle had attempted to join the Confederate Army, but had been told that his eyesight was deficient. The authorities proposed that he build a mill to produce uniforms for the South. There was plenty of locally grown cotton for this purpose. Eager to help the Confederacy any way he could, he agreed. With the defeat, the U.S. Army confiscated the factory. After a great deal of red tape, Earle regained the factory, but died in financial ruin in 1869.

The next major owner of this house was John S. Napier. He and his wife, Mary, had come from Lawrence County, Alabama. As an example of the close relationship of these patrician families, Mary Curtis Myatt Napier was a sister of Aramantha Myatt Fort, W.A. Fort's mother who lived just up the street.

Acquiring the Earle property in 1868, the Napiers undertook major renovation and enlargement of the original house. The result was another Neo-Classical brick house in the growing Waco cityscape. The house has a white wooden portico clear across its front with Ionic columns and ornamental wooden banisters made to resemble the ironwork of New Orleans on both the upper and lower galleries. The shutters are made of cypress.

John S. and Mary C. Napier had seven children. The second oldest daughter, Sarah Arminta, married David Cannon Kinnard, Jr. who hailed from Tennessee. He had served as a chaplain in the Confederate Army. This couple would be the next to occupy the house. It is not definitely known when they moved in, but the 1876 Waco and McLennan County Directory lists the Kinnard's residence. One of their children, Miss Mary Ogilvie Kinnard, would reside in the old home place until her death in 1957.

In 1959, Frances Higginbotham Duncan, later Mrs. George Nalle, of Austin purchased the house and all that remained of the original acreage from the Napier heirs. She completely restored the house and its picket fence. She then enclosed the back porch, added heating and air conditioning, two bath facilities, and furnished it. Several years later, the Texas Highway Department took a considerable amount of the remaining acreage, reducing the original tract to less than half its size. In 1967, Mrs. Nalle presented it to the Waco Perpetual Growth Foundation. Today, it's operated as a house museum by Historic Waco Foundation.

As with so many houses that have survived from the 19th century, Earle-Napier-Kinnard has undergone alterations. Nature herself changed the surroundings of the old house when the 1953 tornado ripped out all the old trees. Somehow, the house itself survived the storm. It stands today—an enduring reminder of days long ago.

EAST TERRACE HOUSE MUSEUM
100 Mill Street

Built by John Wesley Mann around 1873, this handsome baronial mansion perches high above the Brazos River. East Terrace's architectural style differs from our other three Historic Waco Foundation houses. Italianate Villa was a popular architectural style in the Hudson River area, which was the childhood home of Mrs. Mann.

Italianate Villa style is almost always two story. Windows are tall, narrow, and commonly arched at the top. A square cupola or tower is another element common to this style. It had begun in England as a reaction to the formal classical ideals in art and architecture that had been fashionable for 200 years. Though much of the style was borrowed from the informal, rambling Italian farmhouse with its characteristic square towers, it was quickly Americanized.

We know that Neo-Classical style was popular in the South for another decade after it was considered outdated in the East. The builders of Earle-Napier-Kinnard, Fort House, and McCulloch House had come from the South, so it was natural that they had chosen Neo-Classical style for their new Waco homes.

Mr. Mann indulged his wife in her desire for Italiante Villa style. According to her wishes, East Terrace was given a stylish Mansard roof, tall hooded windows and that square Italian cupola on top. The name of Francois Mansard, a 17th century French architect, was given to this type of roof. Ideally, the slope of a mansard roof, from eaves to ridge, is broken into two portions, the lower one slanting at an almost vertical angle. The architectural style of East Terrace has little in common with our other HWF houses, other than the bricks, which were made from the the Brazos river sand.

Even in those early days of Waco, there were several brick yards here. Mr. Mann owned a brick yard, which was located on Dallas Street. He always had his workmen put aside the most perfect bricks for his own home, the terraces, storm cellar, and large chimneys of East Terrace. Today, the storm cellar is the only original outbuilding to survive.

As with all the HWF houses, East Terrace has been altered over the years. The Manns added the dining room and large bedroom above it about 1880. The second addition—the entertainment wing with its own entrance hall—was added in 1884.

Actually, the most dramatic changes of East Terrace were wrought by the Brazos River. Time and time again, renegade flood waters of the Brazos would wash out the terraces. In the disastrous 1913 flood, the waters reached the second floor galleries.

John Wesley Mann was born in Lebanon, Tennessee. In 1858 while on a trip to Waco to buy horses and land, he and his brother, Thomas, settled here. In 1861, he enlisted in the Confederate Army as a private in Company C, the Sixth Regiment, Texas Cavalry. He served as a scout leader under Captain Pete Ross until discharged in 1863.

Returning to Waco after the war, he developed a Midas touch as a businessman. He owned a brick yard, flour mill, refrigeration company, and many other businesses. He served as President of the First National Bank in 1890. The Mann brick kiln furnished half of the bricks for the new suspension bridge, opened in 1870. Mr. Mann died in 1909.

Cemira Twaddle Mann came to Waco as a child from her birthplace, Pough-keepsie, New York. She graduated from Waco Female College and through mutual friends, met John Wesley Mann. They had two sons, Howard and John Wesley, Jr. After she was widowed, Mrs. Mann continued to live at East Terrace for several more years. She then moved to live with her younger son, John Wesley, Jr. on Wild Air Stock Farm near Robinson, Texas. She died in 1934.

As with so many other aging Victorian houses, East Terrace no longer served as a family home. Into the 1930s, it was used as a sanitorium and boarding facility. The old place then lay mouldering and abandoned for years until purchased by Young

Brothers Contractors in the 1950s. At that time, their company headquarters joined the East Terrace property. After Young Brothers generously deeded East Terrace to the Heritage Society of Waco, the house was restored by Waco citizens and the Cooper Foundation. It is now overseen by Historic Waco Foundation.

One little anecdote about East Terrace concerns a conversation between F. M. Young and Bobbie Barnes. She once told me that she had approached him about the amount of dust that was seeping under the closed windows of East Terrace. "We just can't keep our house clean because of all the dust that your crushing machine next door is causing. Mr. Young, what do you suggest we do?" He considered the problem for a moment and then said, "Well, I guess we'll just have to move the crushing machine." And he did.

FORT HOUSE MUSEUM
503 South Fourth

Family history is an integral part of any house, and the names of William and Dionitia Fort will always be associated with Fort House. Like the other three house museums that are operated by Historic Waco Foundation, Fort was built just after the Civil War and in the same part of town, so the folks all knew each other.

Waco Village was a very small community just about the time of the Civil War. Around 2,200 McLennan County men fought in the war, a large number considering the sparse population at that time. All four of the original families were Confederate sympathizers, and all of their men served in that cause. The Civil War devastated the South and Waco was no exception.

As the Texians attempted to return to peace and pick up the threads of their lives, many would bitterly recall the warnings of Sam Houston. Visiting Waco just before Texas was to vote to join the Confederacy, he had predicted that the South could never prevail against the North. To their dismay, the survivors found that they would have to live under U.S. Army occupation for ten years. Times must have been difficult during those Reconstruction days.

William Aldredge Fort had arrived in Waco before the Civil War. He was from La Grange, Alabama where he had farmed until 1850 when he entered into a mercantile partnership with W. W. Downs. In 1853, the two men came to Texas, prospecting for new land. Those were the days when Americans burned with the pioneer fever to head west for new prospects. Young Fort purchased a plantation outside Waco and turned his hand to farming.

In 1862, Fort joined Company D, the First Texas Regiment which would later become Hood's Brigade. He served as a nursing assistant, later promoted to sargeant's rank as a pharmacist's mate. Returning to Waco after the war, he quickly realized that the world of finance would offer more opportunities than farming. He became the first president of the Waco National Bank and was one of the original investors of the company that built the Waco Suspension Bridge in 1870. He was a well-known businessman and a highly respected community leader. At the time of his death, he was a trustee of the Methodist Female College.

Fort had married Dionitia Elizabeth Wilson in l856 and they had four children. His sister, Martha Sandal Fort, had married William Pinkney Downs, son of Fort's old friend, W.W. Downs. The two couples had traveled together to Texas. Later, when the Downs couple died of typhoid fever, the Forts took in their three orphaned children. The Fort household must have been a lively one.

The house that William A. Fort built for his family in 1868 reflected his deep South origins. The Greek Revival or Neo-classical style that he chose for his new home was dominant from about 1830-1850. It was an architectural statement that symbolized Greek democracy, rejecting our traditional ties to England. Greek Revival remained popular in the South well into the 1860s.

By definition, Greek Revival adheres to symmetry since the ancient Greeks always sought harmony and balance in their architecture. Fort House is a perfect example of this style. Constructed of local brick, the house is designed so that all rooms on both floors enjoy cross ventilation. Twin fluted Ionic columns made of cypress flank the double front door set in the middle of the house front. A handsome gable roof that tops the capitals is reminiscent of a Greek temple.

Fort had purchased the land—about six acres—from his wife, Dionitia. He built barns, put in orchards, and planted gardens. This large family and the servant staff were supplied with most of their needs from this little farm. Fort's elderly mother, Aramantha Harlow Myatt Fort, was a sister of Mary Curtis Myatt Napier who lived just down the street. Because of her age and delicate health, the old lady was given the best room in the house, the downstairs' bedroom. A thoughtful son, Fort was also a very provident father, sending all the boys off to Virginia Military Institute and his niece and daughter to Wesleyan Female Institute in Staunton, Virginia.

A house, like a family, changes over the years and Fort House would undergo several changes as it aged. In 1876, the ell of the house was elongated to add two bedrooms on the upper floor and a kitchen and a three-walled room on the first floor. This same addition contained a breezeway, kitchen, and a storehouse that was open on one end so that the wagons could pull through to disgorge the provisions. The open breezeway that connected the dining room to the originally detached kitchen was enclosed around the turn of the century.

At age 52, William Aldredge Fort died, a relatively young man, in 1878. Mrs. Fort lived well into the early 20th century. Three generations of Forts now sleep in the family plot in Oakwood Cemetery. The Fort House committee recently cleaned and restored the handsome old tombstones and their surrounding marble enclosure.

After both Forts were gone, the building was sold to be used as a boarding house with all that implies. The railroad had come through and by early 20th century, the neighborhood was no longer fashionable. All Waco was moving westward. Rooms were cut up and the front balcony, which originally was attached to the columns, was mutilated. An awkward addition was made to the front left side of the house. In 1956, Waco Junior League purchased the neglected old place and restored it to its current state. The title was finally turned over to Historic Waco Foundation, which operates it today as Fort House Museum.

The house has very little of the original Fort family furnishings, but it is filled with handsome 19th century furniture. Every so often, a photograph or a letter will drift back from some family member. Just recently, an out-of-state descendant happened to come across our HWF website. Remembering that he had several silver monogrammed spoons that had once belonged to the Forts, he generously donated them to Historic Waco Foundation. Two of the original dining chairs were recently returned by a family descendant.

The Fort family still thrives in Texas. Several years ago, the Forts held a family reunion here in Waco and everyone was invited to a lemonade party at Fort House. More than fifty adults and children from all over Texas visited, curious about their forebears. Fort House docents poured iced lemonade and gave tours all afternoon. It was a fine event and everyone was satisfied that the old house was being looked after with loving care.

HOFFMANN HOUSE
810 South Fourth Street

In 1986, Clark Concrete Company offered Historic Waco Foundation a gift of a graceful Queen Anne house at 1921 Webster Street in the neighborhood known as Bell's Hill. Our organization was in need of an office building and this seemed like the answer. After moving the abandoned old building to its present location on South Fourth Street next door to Earle-Napier-Kinnard House Museum, it was thoroughly renovated and furnished in modern style.

Hoffmann House is now used as corporate offices for Historic Waco Foundation. A snug little cottage trimmed with Victorian gingerbread, it's a style that was popular in the United States from 1880-1910. Some of the identifying features of a Queen Anne house are steeply-pitched roof lines, usually with a dominant front-facing gable, patterned shingles, bay windows and an asymmetrical facade with a partial or wrap-around porch. The style could be adapted to multi-storied houses or scaled down to cottage size.

Many of these features can be seen in the one-story Hoffmann House—the steeply pitched roof, a bay window across the front, the wrap-around porch and the decorative shingle trim. It is a classic Queen Anne, made even more so by its teal blue exterior paint color. They were typically painted in bright clear colors with contrasting trim.

The interior of Hoffmann House is no longer as it was originally. Even so, the rooms are finished with similar decorative trim or gingerbread that is seen on the exterior of the house. The entrance hall stained glass window, with its pastel hues, is original. Such windows were quite common in Queen Anne houses.

The house was named for the family that had lived there in the first half of the 20th century. William Herman Hoffmann, born in St. Louis, Missouri, had come to Waco in 1885. He and his family moved to the little cottage in 1907. Mr. Hoffmann held several positions with Waco businesses and served on the boards of many civic institutions.

The family consisted of wife Ellie, son Harry who worked at Goldstein-Migel Department Store, and daughters Fay and Bird. Many Wacoans today remember the two flamboyant sisters who brought dance and drama to our town. It was Fay and Bird who put the Hoffmann name before the public.

Having studied dance with Mrs. Hart who taught at Waco Female College on Fifth Street, the two girls realized that dance was to be their future. Mrs. Hoffmann had encouraged them to study, paying for the lessons with her buttermilk and egg money. The girls followed Mrs. Hart to her school in Dallas where they studied to be dance teachers.

About 1908, Fay and Bird (sometimes known as Baby) returned to Waco to open a dance studio in Woodmen Hall between Fourth and Fifth Streets on Austin Avenue. Still in their teens in 1917, they taught ballroom dancing to soldiers from Camp MacArthur. It was the soldiers who nicknamed the girls "Hoffmannettes."

For small town Waco, the attractive sisters must have seemed like exotic birds. They loved to dress in an eccentric, but fashionable manner. They may have been flamboyant, but they taught dance to three generations of Waco youngsters and their recitals were always popularly received.

The Hoffmanns loved to travel and always took their mother, Ellie, with them. She was an elegant person and they dearly loved her. Ellie played the piano for practice sessions, and one of her pianos is still there in a reception room that used to be the dance studio at Hoffmann House.

The ladies continued to teach dance almost to the time of Bird's death in 1966. Fay died in a nursing home in 1972, thereby ending a colorful era in Waco's cultural history. A memorial dedication was held on May 1, 1973 at Oakwood Cemetery honoring the two Hoffmann sisters who had contributed so much to their community.

McCULLOCH HOUSE MUSEUM
407 Columbus Avenue

O f all the Historic Waco Foundation restored houses, McCulloch House, built in 1872, had deteriorated the most. It was the last Victorian building brought into the family of HWF's four restored house museums.

The last family member had died in 1971 and it was abandoned shortly thereafter. Vagrants broke down the front door and began to camp there. They ripped up moldings, mantles, and loose floorboards to burn for firewood in the fireplaces. In no time, it was stripped clean—a ghostly old skeleton that no one wanted.

Only Mrs. Maurice (Bobbie) Barnes frantically fought for its salvation, undeterred by many delays and desperate to begin restoration. She always seemed to have a special affection for McCulloch, most likely because she had fought so hard to save the old wreck.

The house actually began as a simple two-room structure, built by Dr. Josiah Hatcher Caldwell, who hailed from Green County, Kentucky. He had served as a medical officer for the Confederacy in the Missouri 16th Infantry. At war's end, he and his family moved to Waco where he practiced medicine and served as McLennan County physician. In 1866, Dr. Caldwell bought the Columbus Avenue property at public auction for $500 in gold and built his house with a detached kitchen. His wife was Maria Anderson of Cerulean Springs, Kentucky. The couple had five children. Caldwell died in 1896.

The Caldwell homestead cottage can be seen on the east side of the main building. This building was composed of two rooms with front and back entrances, as well as a sturdy fireplace in each room. It may have been a tight fit for Dr. Caldwell and his family, but it would have been considered substantial living quarters for those Reconstruction era days when most Wacoans were living in dirt floor log cabins.

In 1872, Champe Carter McCulloch purchased the land and cottage from Caldwell for $600. He built a handsome Greek revival home of rosy brick, incorporating the Caldwell structure into the grand plan and connecting the detached kitchen on the opposite corner. Four tall Doric columns were erected across the mansion's front with both an upstairs and downstairs gallery. The house had an unobstructed view of the river and Waco's new suspension bridge, which opened January l, 1870.

Champe Carter McCulloch was born in Westwood, St. Clair County, Missouri. He served as captain of the 2nd Cavalry Brigade, Missouri State Guard CSA. On his return to Waco, he married Emma Bassett, daughter of Louis Bassett of Alabama. McCulloch opened a grocery business in Waco in 1876 and proved to be a successful businessman. He was elected Mayor of Waco and served in that capacity for eleven years. The McCullochs were the parents of ten children with only seven surviving to adulthood. He died in 1907 and his widow lived in the house until her death in 1929.

McCulloch House was a family residence for a century. Four of the McCulloch children grew to adulthood, went off to school and left home to marry or pursue careers. Son Louis Bassett McCulloch and his wife, Lucy J. Pickens Morris, lived there until the 1953 tornado.

This tornado devastated downtown Waco and McCulloch house was not spared. The entire roof was blown away and rain poured into the house. Louis died in 1958 and his widow, Lucy J. Pickens McCulloch, returned in 1960 to live there until her death in 1971. Bravely, she boarded off the upstairs and attempted to live on the first floor. Piece after piece of original furnishings were sold off in public sales. The gallant old lady died penniless and the house fell into disuse.

Some original furnishings have been returned by those who must have purchased them from Lucy McCulloch. One donor returned a silver tea service given to Adelle McCulloch by her father. It's now prominently displayed in the dining room. The old family Bible in the front parlor was given by the descendants of Champe Carter McCulloch with the proviso that they may enter future family births, weddings, and deaths.

DECORATIVE ARTS

THE ANTIMACASSAR: A VICTORIAN NECESSITY

W hat is an antimacassar? The word simply reeks with Victorian antediluvian (belonging to the period before the Flood) prissiness. Actually, antimacassars were a very practical idea that solved a household problem.

During the 19th and early 20th centuries, the gentleman's fashion for heavily-oiled hair became quite popular. Supposedly, the oil was imported from Macassar, a seaport on the island of Celebes in what is now Indonesia. The exotically named oil most likely consisted of palm oil with a few sweet-smelling additions.

Macassar oil was sold in deeply-embossed square glass bottles with such extravagant claims as an advertisement in the June, 1812 *Edinburgh Advertiser:* "A preparation for eradicating all impurities of the hair, increasing its growth where there once was baldness." Their Royal Highnesses the Princess of Wales and Duke of Sussex endorsed this miracle product—a common practice among the English nobles, even today.

The popular concoction even found its way into the literature of the time. Macassar oil was mentioned in Lewis Carroll's *Through the Looking-Glass* as well as Lord Byron's *Don Juan* when he says, "In Virtues nothing earthly could surpass her…save thine incomparable oil, Macassar!"

The word *'antimacassar'* entered the English lexicon around mid-century, coined by some anonymous housewife, desperate to preserve her upholstered furniture from oil stains. These dainty doilies would absorb the hair oil and could easily be removed to bleach and launder.

Most antimacassar doilies were hand-crocheted—a needle art with which most Victorian women were familiar.

Those were the days when a housewife always had a piece of handwork going. As was said, "Idle fingers are the devil's workshop." Lavish crochet designs developed; and soon, every chair back was decorated with lacy crochet work. Matching sets of three that included doilies for armrests became quite popular. Commercially produced doilies were available through stores and catalog houses and small curved pins were specially designed to hold them in place.

In the latter part of the 19th century, theaters began to use antimacassars to preserve their upholstered seats. The idea eventually caught on with public transportation. Seat headrests on trains, buses, and even 20th century aircraft were covered with sanitary disposable paper antimacassars, which could be changed with each passenger.

As an afterthought, look around your own parlor. I'll bet you have at least one upholstered armchair outfitted with the remnant of the antimacassar idea. Today's upholsterers always give those small removable arm coverlets in the matching fabric.

THE BARNES DECORATIVE ARTS COURSE

It all began in the 1930s when Dr. Maurice Barnes and his young wife, Bobbie, traveled to New York City. He was to study surgery there. Someone suggested to Bobbie that she might be interested in studying at the Metropolitan Museum. She was especially attracted to its American Decorative Arts wing.

For three years, Bobbie attended weekly lectures on the history of American architecture and the decorative arts. Later, she would reminisce about visiting many of the city's early Dutch houses, most of which have since disappeared. She also visited Colonial Williamsburg in Virginia and Winterthur in Delaware.

The New York City experience had such a profound impact on Bobbie that the decorative arts became her lifetime passion. Returning to Waco after Maurice had finished his studies, she began to see Waco through new eyes. She saw that much of our architectural past was quickly disappearing, and she agonized over every historic structure that was lost to the wrecker's ball. With other historians such as Roger Conger, she founded Historic Waco Foundation.

Ultimately, four Victorian houses were saved and restored: Fort House, Earle-Napier-Kinnard, East Terrace, and McCulloch House. Later, the little Queen Anne house where the Hoffmann family once lived was given to HWF and moved to its present location on Fourth Street. Today, it serves as HWF offices.

Bobbie Barnes quickly perceived that the members of each house board would need special instruction in the decorative arts if they were to be able to give knowledgeable tours. Her Lavonia Jenkins Barnes Decorative Arts course, begun 45 years ago, was a resounding success. During the first decade or so, there was always a waiting list of applicants.

Believing that travel is a good way to educate, Bobbie began to plan small tours for Wacoans. They went to Natchez, Charleston, Savannah, Washington, Philadelphia, the Pennsylvania German country, Boston, Nantucket Island, and the restored 17th century Sturbridge Village in Massachusetts.

Then, they ventured overseas to visit the great country houses of England, Scotland, Ireland, France, and Italy. Bobbie was a tireless traveler with an all-consuming interest in her favorite subject and a desire to share it with others. She was active in several national decorative arts organizations and through them, began to develop invaluable entrée to some of the most exclusive places.

"*Just as time and civilizations are evaluated through shards, so may man's social history and development be traced through architecture. In such studies one comes to understand why and how homes were built in a particular style and why they reflect certain trends.*"
— Lavonia Jenkins Barnes,
   Early Homes of Waco

Bobbie Barnes in the parlor of the McCulloch House before its restoration, late 1970s.

For instance, she told me that every time she traveled to New York City, she always visited the Frick Gallery. She would be invited by the director to take tea upstairs in the parlor of Henry Clay Frick, a 19th century steel magnate and the founder of the Frick Gallery.

I remember one European trip that Bobbie described to me. She recalled, "On one of our French tours of about eight people, I had arranged beforehand for a special visit to the palace of Versailles. Our little tour bus arrived at the locked front gates early one morning. A sign said, 'Closed,' but we waited and the caretaker came out to unlock the great wrought iron gates. We drove onto the palatial grounds of the home of the Sun King, Louis XIV."

The caretaker gave the group the usual tour of some of the more important ground floor rooms. Without the usual chatter of other tour directors, the place was strangely quiet. Then the caretaker said, "I have something special I want to share with you. Come upstairs!" They all ascended a great marble staircase and the caretaker led them to a door, which he unlocked. It was a small workshop, not much bigger than a closet.

Bobbie remembered the caretaker's telling the group, "This is the room where Louis XVI occasionally came to escape the tedium of court life. In complete privacy, he and an old clock maker friend would work on such mechanical devices as clocks and locks. You are privileged to see this humble space where France's last Bourbon king spent his leisure hours. Nothing has been touched since the day when he was taken away by the revolutionists, never to return."

In the beginning, Bobbie delivered all her decorative arts course lectures. Then, she began to invite outside experts to speak on such subjects as silver, carpets, architecture. But there was one lecture that Bobbie retained for herself. All the other lectures could be done by others, but Bobbie dearly loved to talk about the early American furniture that she had originally studied at the Metropolitan Museum in her youth.

I believe that it was the year 2003 that I was chairman of the Barnes course. I called Bobbie and asked if I could count on her to give the Jacobean/William & Mary lecture. I knew she was in failing health, so I assured her that I would help arrange her slides and re-type her lecture in large print. She agreed.

Every day for a couple of weeks, I buzzed over to her place and we would study together in her library. A tuna sandwich and coffee for a lunch break and then, back to work. Finally, I had all the slides organized and her lecture in good order and re-typed.

The day before her lecture, she phoned with the earth-shattering news. "Claire, I feel so awful, I just can't do it. You'll have to do it for me." Frantic, I argued, but she insisted. "After all, you have been learning it all along. It's all there for you, I know you can do it." And so that is how I "inherited" the Jacobean/William & Mary lecture. The evening as I delivered it, I taped it and had her evaluate it for me the next day. She approved. In her honor, I've given that particular Barnes lecture ever since.

Bobbie is gone now and I think of her every year that I speak about Jacobean/William & Mary furniture. I must admit that I have grown very fond of the subject myself. The homely, utilitarian furniture of that period says so much about our early colonial ancestors.

BUTTER: ONE OF NATURE'S LITTLE MIRACLES

When I was a little girl visiting my Speegleville grandmother, I loved to watch her butter-making ceremony. She always seemed to imbue the process with a serious, concentrated approach. Pulling out her earthenware churn with its vertical dasher, she would fill it with rich cream from her favorite milk cow, a dainty little Jersey with big brown eyes. Then, she would sit and begin the up-and-down movement of the wooden dasher. Getting into the swing, she might even break out in one of her favorite hymns—Rock of Ages—encouraging me to join in the sing fest. Her movements would become slower and more labored as the butter began to "make."

Finally, it was time. She never clocked her work; she just knew from long experience when the butter was ready. Removing the lid, she would scoop up all the butter that had risen to the top and set it into a big bowl. The residue was buttermilk, a favorite drink of mine. Setting the bowl of butter under the kitchen tap, she would proceed to "wash" it. This was a vitally important step in the process of butter-making.

Sloshing the butter around with fresh cold tap water, she slowly worked out all the residual milk. Without this step in the butter-making process, her butter would have been ruined by the milk, which would have quickly soured. A good housewife was always concerned with the sweetness of her butter.

Grandmother's place was called Four Oaks Farm. At her direction, a Waco printer had designed a big square of oiled paper with that name printed on the top. Each block of butter that emerged from her one-pound mold would be carefully wrapped in a Four Oaks Farm paper and then given to friends or sold to folks all around Speegleville.

There have been several popular types of butter churns in the past. One of the most intriguing is the Davis Swing Churn, patented in 1879 and manufactured by Vermont Farm Machine Co. of Bellows Falls, Vermont. We have a good example of one on display in the Fort House 19th century kitchen. It consists of a wooden body that sets horizontally in a sturdy cross-bar stand. We know from research that Davis Swing Churns were available in twelve sizes, from seven gallons to 300-gallon capacity, and were always painted buttercup yellow.

Cream would be poured into the top opening and the churning would be achieved by a horizontal swinging motion. This particular style of Davis Swing Churn could have produced up to twelve pounds of butter. The remaining buttermilk was drained out through a small plughole in the bottom of the churn. This rustic gadget may seem clumsy, but I can imagine that it was fairly efficient for its purpose.

One amusing sidelight to the Davis Swing Churn was an extra fixture, a treadmill that could be ordered through the company catalog. Attached to the churn, the power to move the treadmill was provided by a large dog or goat. One would wonder about the efficiency of such a contraption.

The most popular design was Grandmother's vertical style churn. We have a fine example of this style in the Fort House kitchen. It is classic gray earthenware with two blue decorative rings. Marked 'Marshall Pottery Co. Marshall, Texas,' this size could have contained up to four gallons of cream. Marshall Pottery Co. was founded in 1895 and is still in existence. It was given to us by house member Ed Dvoracek.

A third style was a small contraption called a Dazey churn. You see these in antique stores quite often. The Dazey is relatively modern in time, the company having been formed after the turn of the 20th century. It usually had a heavy glass body and was meant to set on a table or counter as the person turned the metal-handled dasher. With its molded glass body, it must have been quite handy to use and easy to clean.

In the 19th century, folks had no knowledge of the dangers of cholesterol. The word was yet to come into common usage. Everyone ate lots of butter and used it in their baking. Fort House overlooked a working farm with orchards, animal barns, and gardens. They would have had several milk cows to provide all the necessary milk to make butter. Of course, not everyone had a cow, so it was quite common for butter to be used for barter. One elderly woman could remember that her grandmother always traded one pound of butter to her grandchild's music teacher for weekly music lessons.

The Fort family, with their seven children and large staff of house and farm workers, would have consumed prodigious amounts of butter. We know from having read surviving family letters that it was common for the Forts to entertain twenty guests for dinner. A churn such as this Davis Swing Churn would have been kept busy churning out butter for everyone.

EASTLAKE STYLE

In the world of 19th century decorative arts, the name Eastlake looms large. Charles Locke Eastlake (1833-1906) was an English architect who made a great impact on the decorative arts of that time, both in England and the United States.

His philosophy was described in his *Hints on Household Taste in Furniture, Upholstery, and Other Details*, a book first published in 1868. It would undergo six more editions within the next eleven years and is still in print today. In his preface, he stated that his object was "to suggest some fixed principles of taste for the popular guidance of those who are not accustomed to hear such principles defined."

This arbiter of the decorative arts made no furniture himself, but his design ideas were replicated by professional cabinetmakers. The Eastlake style became immensely popular. Nearly every middle-class household in this country must have had at least one piece of Eastlake-inspired furniture. Unfortunately, many design travesties were committed in his name. In the fourth revision of his book in 1878, he complained that his ideas were being translated into cheap, ungraceful furniture.

Eastlake was from a mildly-distinguished English family. He had received a classical education, developing a natural talent for drawing and painting. Awarded a medal for architectural drawings in 1854, he entered the Royal Academy to study architecture. Three years of travel in Europe broadened his knowledge of painting, sculpture, and architecture. He never would practice architecture, but devoted his talents to designing furniture, wallpaper, interior fittings, metalwork, and jewelry.

As a student, Eastlake fell in love with medieval buildings. He pronounced it "Poetry in stone, the Gothic tradition that left a native English style in domestic architecture and furniture from the 15th and 16th centuries." He also admired the directness and simplicity of Jacobean furniture from 17th century England.

His furniture designs had a simple look. He promoted angular, notched, carved, and distinctly rectilinear construction, believing it to be strong and honest. Studying his wallpaper designs, you can detect the influence of William Morris' philosophy of the Arts & Crafts style of that same era. The two men were contemporaries and their design philosophies were quite similar.

An insular Englishman, Eastlake quite naturally disdained 18th century French furniture and described its many 19th century ornate revival styles as "bad, vicious, and extravagant in principle." He detested all those voluptuous French curved backs and dancing legs.

His strictest principle of design was that "every material used in art manufacture is obviously restricted by the nature of its substance to certain conditions of form. The general treatment of materials such as glass, metal, stone should always follow the form of the raw material. If the material of which a piece is composed is honestly treated, there is no reason why it should not be as picturesque as any other piece."

Eastlake thought it a weakness that each craft tended to develop its own style. He taught that a talented craftsman or artist should be familiar with all the areas of design. "The same spirit of life and vigor that animates the blacksmith's forge should do likewise to the sculptor's studio and the haberdasher's shop."

Studying the table of contents of *Hints on Household Taste*, you can see that Eastlake had strong opinions on just about every aspect of architecture and the decorative arts. Furniture, floors, wall treatments, art, crockery, table glass, plate, cutlery, women's clothes, jewelry, stoneware, metalwork, and etiquette are all discussed in his popular treatise.

One of the foremost proponents of the Eastlake style in the U.S. was the 19th century American architect, Henry Hobson Richardson. The furniture he designed for several public libraries back east are similar to illustrations from Eastlake's book.

Charles Eastlake ended his career as Keeper and Secretary of the National Gallery of England. During his period of office, he rearranged and classified all the paintings in the collection. Through his writings and lectures, he made his advocates more aware of good taste and more critical of their surroundings.

There are several Eastlake-style pieces in HWF house museums. East Terrace boasts a dignified Eastlake pier mirror, 1884, in its entrance hall. Made of walnut with burl veneer, it has the typical ball and stick spindles and a small table surface of brown marble. It is original to the Mann family who lived there at East Terrace.

Eastlake dining chair

Across the river at Fort House, there is a set of walnut dining room chairs, 1880, with leather upholstery. They have fanciful carving, rather ornate for Eastlake, but Eastlake nevertheless. Up Fourth Street at McCulloch House sits an Eastlake rectangular walnut side table, 1885, with a pedestal base and porcelain casters.

All this Eastlake-style Victorian furniture in our houses reflects the time frame of his influence, mid-1800s to the end of that century. Eastlake's little handbook, filled with his hints on household taste, is his enduring legacy to the decorative arts.

EVER-POPULAR SPODE

What's blue and white and beautiful all over? Spode dinnerware! Historic Waco Foundation is the recipient of a gift of more than 100 pieces of handsome blue-on-white Spode dinnerware. This includes eight place settings with a teapot, butter dish, and several covered serving dishes, which are displayed in the newly created Fort House 19th century kitchen. The donor, Lori Phillips (who previously lived in England,) fell in love with this particular pattern and hand-picked each piece from the factory at Stoke-on-Trent.

Companies such as Spode, Wedgwood, and others had built their factories there in the 18th century because of the area's profusion of high-quality clay deposits. Earthenware is the lowest grade of three types of ceramic composition from Spode factories. This donated dinnerware is not old, but the pattern, named Blue Italian, goes back to 1816, so it's appropriate to exhibit it in a Victorian setting. Its romantic, classical landscape is still in production today. The shape of the plate edge is called Camilla Cottage design.

John Bedford writes in his *Old Spode China* that Blue Italian is Spode's most famous and long-lived pattern. "It fully deserves its fame and persistence, for it is a real masterpiece of its kind. There is no doubt that, in their class, Spode's blue-printed transferwares represent some of the finest craftsmanship of the day. The Spode engravers had really learnt their job, and the striking *chiaroscuro* effects in the painted Chinese subjects of other patterns are here far surpassed." (*Chiaroscuro* refers to the distribution of light and shade in a picture.)

The term "transferware" entails the use of designs engraved on tissue that were "transferred" to the wet, blank earthenware plate (or cup, saucer, etc.) In his *"Antique Blue and White Spode,"* Sydney Williams describes this transfer technique. "The copper plate that has been engraved with the design is heated and the color (a mixture of pigment and oil) is worked into the channels of the plate. All superfluous color is then wiped off. The surface of the copper plate, being free from color substance, will not print, but forms the white portions of the print. A sheet of prepared tissue-paper made wet with a solution of soap and water is carefully laid, without any wrinkles, onto the surface of the copper plate. Both are then passed through the rollers of a press. The copperplate is then heated to enable the tissue-paper to be peeled off."

He added, "The tissue is then applied to the white body of the ware, which is in its unfinished 'biscuit' stage. Scissors are used to pare away all superfluous paper when the design is applied or transferred to the unglazed ware. The tissue is then rubbed with a ball pad and lubricated with soap. The ware is next immersed in a tub of water and the tissue paper floats off, leaving the oil-printed design fused on the ware. The piece is then dipped in a clear glaze and passed into the glost oven where the firing gives the piece its final finish."

Blue—extracted from cobalt—was the easiest hue to use in this process and is the most common color for transferware. In the early days, intensity of color could vary slightly and it took much experimentation before other colors such as red, green, black, and brown were successfully used in this transfer method.

Because of the popularity of transferware, every potter in Staffordshire sought to develop a similar ware. It was made with dozens of scenes, many with exotic, oriental subjects. All through the 18th century, artists had traveled to foreign lands. Their etchings inspired many of the dinnerware designs that are still collected today. There are transferware patterns based on ancient Italy, Greece, China, India, and the Middle East. The knowledgeable collector easily distinguishes one from another.

One of the most popular was the Willow pattern that was inspired by a Chinese design. First made by Thomas Turner at the Caughley Pottery Works in Shropshire, no other pattern has been more copied than the Willow.

The Prince of Wales, who ruled England as regent, 1811-1820, visited the Spode Works in 1806. An avid collector and a devoted fan of the decorative arts, he was especially interested in Spode's products. As a result of this visit, Josiah Spode II was appointed "Potter to His Royal Highness the Prince of Wales." A service was designed for the Regent with his symbol worked into the design. For his coronation as George IV in 1821, a second Spode service was created in his honor.

FINE RUGS WITH A FRENCH ACCENT

L a Belle France has always been known for her superior tapestries and carpets, famous throughout the world since the 14th century. Tapestry's origins can be traced to the arrival of Flemish weavers who sought refuge in Aubusson around 1580. Rug weaving was first introduced to Europe through Spain when much of the Iberian Peninsula was under the control of Muslim Moors from the 8th century to the 13th century. In France, there are two rug manufacturers from the 17th and 18th centuries whose reputations tower above all others: Aubusson and Savonnerie.

The city of Aubusson is located in central France and is the seat of a school of decorative arts and a museum devoted to the history of French tapestries. Aubusson rugs were first made there around 1665. Their designs are still being copied by countries such as India, Pakistan, China, and Iran.

There is a lovely old Aubusson rug that can be seen upstairs on the landing at McCulloch House Museum. The design is a center medallion with floral motifs. Typically, the Aubusson palette of colors is pastel, and the main body of this rug is

pale pink. Dated around 1870, our rug must have been one of the last produced since the factory closed in that decade. It is now very faded and has a worn edge, but we treasure it because of the noble history that it represents. It was given to Historic Waco Foundation by Mr.and Mrs. William P. Davis.

The difference between Aubusson and Savonnerie is easily determined. Basically, the Aubusson is a flat weave, akin to today's kilims of the Middle East. Aubusson weavers didn't tie off the threads so that the underside of their rugs is a mass of loose threads.

46

Another feature of the Aubusson is that the weavers used the "slit" weave technique. When two colors butted up against each other, a barely discernible slit in the rug was the result.

On the other hand, the Savonnerie is a lush pile rug. They were woven so that all the knots were tied and woven in, similar to Persian rugs. Sometimes, the surface of the finished rug was slightly cut or sculptured around the patterns in order to achieve a certain dimension. Originally, Savonnerie manufactured its product in a large warehouse where *savon* (the French word for soap) had once been made, hence the name Savonnerie. Located in Paris, it was set up by Pierre Dupont in 1628 under the royal patronage of Henri IV himself.

Savonnerie rugs, many of which were quite large, were produced under the direction of artists of the royal court and were mainly woven for palaces and to fill special orders. The Sun King, Louis XIV, quite often would send another monarch a royal gift of a Savonnerie rug. This was his diplomatic way of displaying the superior products of French craftsmen. The most prolific period for these rugs was between 1650 and 1789. Like so many other art forms, production was interrupted by the French Revolution at the end of the century.

What made the rug industry of Aubusson and Savonnerie unique is that the French craftsmen succeeded in an art that has always been practiced in the Middle East, Persia, and China. The work is so labor intensive that ambitious rug operations, which began in England, for instance, never succeeded. It just wasn't practical. Somehow, it succeeded in France.

As a sidelight, some people are confused as to the difference in meaning of rug and carpet. According to Hugh Henson, who gives the annual HWF Barnes Decorative Arts lecture on rugs, "In our country, little distinction is made between the two words; they are interchangeable. The English, though, consider anything smaller than 6' x 9' to be a rug. Larger pieces are called carpets."

RETURNED TO VERSAILLES

Some years ago, Versailles was undergoing its biggest renovation since the Revolution. The director of the project—a man named Van der Kempe—just happened to be at a Manhattan dinner party, chatting with a wealthy American woman. She commended him for his work at Versailles. Van der Kempe told her that he was searching for a large carpet for one of its reception rooms. "You know, madame, you own such a carpet, a Savonnerie, original to Versailles. It is here in New York, in storage." The American, the owner of an enormous collection, realized that she didn't even know of its existence. "Oh, then you must take it. It is my gift to Versailles!"

THE FLOOR CLOTH OF EAST TERRACE

During the year 2007, Historic Waco Foundation commissioned world-renowned conservator Robert Alden Marshall to study the interior of one of Waco's most prominent Victorian house museums, East Terrace. His evaluation was generously funded through a grant from the Cooper Foundation.

East Terrace had been built by John Wesley Mann just after the Civil War. Though she grew up in Waco, his wife, Cemira had Yankee roots. Perhaps this caused her to have decorating ideas that differed so greatly from that of her neighbors. Evidence of her sophisticated taste can be seen in the architectural style she chose for her new home.

Conservator Marshall spent several weeks scraping small areas of the cream-colored painted woodwork, walls, doorways, fireplaces, and shutters throughout the house. Under his expert eye, the secrets of East Terrace's original flamboyant color design were revealed.

From Marshall's scientific testing, we now have proof that in its original existence, the East Terrace interior has little in common with its appearance today. True to her Victorian tastes, Cemira finished her new home's walls, mantles, doorways, and floors with splashy color and intricately-textured surfaces. As fresh paint was applied over the 134 years of East Terrace's existence, all its bold design elements and dark woodwork gradually disappeared beneath many layers of bland, neutral color.

Nineteenth century interiors consistently displayed bold styles. We know that Victorians were fond of splashy wallpapers, upholstery, and carpets. Many surviving rooms from that era swirl with complex pattern and vivid color. As with East Terrace, many a Victorian home lost its original features to a modern makeover.

One day—working on a hunch—Marshall made a most enticing discovery. Curious, he pulled up a wide wooden threshold located in an upstairs bedroom. A threshold is a raised board that hides an unsightly seam in the floorboards between two rooms. Marshall knew from experience that a threshold sometimes hides fragments of carpeting or some sort of floor covering.

Much to his delight, Marshall discovered a fragment of the original floor cloth that must have originally covered the entire upstairs landing. Basically speaking, a floor cloth is a painted cloth meant to emulate a woven rug. It's an idea that dates back to the 17th century.

Faded and torn, the scrap of cloth still exudes the warmth and exuberance of the late 19th century decorative arts. Its bold combination of red, gold, brown, and cream creates a handsome geometric design, reminiscent of a quilt design.

Two board members of East Terrace, Wendy Buck and Billie Brownfield, worked with me for several months to replicate this floor cloth design (see inside front cover). Previously, I had worked on the two floor cloths for the newly-refurbished Fort House 19th century kitchen, so I have some experience with this sort of project.

Careful analysis shows that ordinary, coarse burlap was the base for the original, but we chose an especially fine grade of canvas. After careful analysis of the original faded colors, slightly brighter shades of acrylic paint were chosen: red, gold, black, brown, and cream. Employing carbon paper, we traced the design on the primed canvas and then, painstakingly hand-painted the geometric design in water-based paint. The corners

were then cut, mitered and all edges glued under. Three separate coats of clear polyurethane ensure an enduring finish.

The three of us worked off and on for almost five months before we accomplished what we believe to be a true replication of the original design. The finished floor cloth has now been set on the floor of the upstairs landing of East Terrace, a reminder that the entire floor was once covered with this colorful, geometrical design.

THE FORT HOUSE 19th CENTURY KITCHEN

It was wonderful! Our grand opening of the Fort House restored kitchen was a decidedly successful event. The old landmark Victorian was filled with guests from all over Texas. Laughter and lively conversation between old and new friends abounded. Mr. and Mrs. Fort would have been pleased to know their home is still a show place, just as it must have been in the 19th century when they resided there.

Yes, it was the kitchen that claimed all the attention. Once a separate room from the house, it was originally linked to the main dining room by an open breezeway. Over the years, the breezeway was bricked in and the kitchen became a part of the house.

In August of 2005, I was asked to lead a committee to do the restoration. It has taken our committee more than a year and a half to complete the task. Our team scoured all central Texas, visiting junkyards, estate sales, and antiques stores. Earnings from many years of annual Fort House Geranium Sales funded this venture, along with generous monetary donations from friends of Fort House. Thousands of volunteer hours were spent to create Historic Waco Foundation's first authentic 19th century kitchen, interpretation period 1870-1900.

The star of the kitchen is an authentic cast-iron, wood-burning cook stove with the necessary pots, water kettle, pans, and skillets. There are two cabinets that once stood in a 19th century central Texas farmhouse: a pie safe and a possum belly cabinet. In the center of the room is a kitchen table with the requisite "spooner," a tall container for spoons. One of our last acquisitions came from Houston, a dry sink where the dishes would have been washed. Water would have been brought in from the outside well and heated on the stove. The removable top of this dry sink is made of copper and holds a dishpan and a bar of homemade soap. Another cabinet was manufactured at the end of the century in Indiana, hence its generic name—Hoosier.

One of our first purchases was a strange-looking device called a Davis Swing Churn. Most of us think of a butter churn as one which is made of earthenware with a vertical plunger, but the wooden body of the Davis churn is set horizontally onto a sturdy cradle. With six gallons of cream inside, the churn was then swung from end to end until the butter "made." Twelve pounds of precious butter was the happy result.

Every significant item in the room has gone through the Collections Committee of HWF. The Committee consists of several knowledgeable people who have carefully guided me in the selection of furnishings for the kitchen. It is through their thoughtfully considered guidance that everything in the Fort House restored kitchen is authentic to the interpretive period.

Researching family history, we are fortunate to have had access to surviving Fort family letters and documents. For instance, we know that it was quite common for the Forts to have entertained up to twenty guests for dinner. The cook and her helpers would have worked hard all day preparing the many snacks and meals for the large family and guests.

The kitchen has always been the heart of a home. In the far-off days of the 19th century, the Fort House kitchen was always a source of warmth in cold winters when upstairs rooms might have been chilly. A pot of coffee must always have been on the stove for any family member or servant who needed a pick-me-up.

Similar to most kitchens, the Fort House kitchen would have been a multiple-use room. All the possibilities were taken into consideration as we slowly furnished the room. Yes, food preparation would have been paramount, but the room would have been used for canning fruit in the summer, ironing the laundry, and the children would have taken their wintertime baths in a #8 washtub next to the warm cook stove. A carpet beater and an old broom from Waco's old broom factory lean

51

against the wall, while a gun sets atop the pie safe just in case a varmint is raising a ruckus in the chicken coop out back some night.

We have tried to give a down-home quality to the room. I sewed its half-curtains of plain unbleached muslin. Two dear little rag-rugs were hand-crocheted by committee member Doris Gage. Several of us created two painted floor cloths that emulate old-fashioned linoleum. In colors of cream, blue, and green, we painted stripes and checks to make handsome floor coverings for both kitchen and breezeway (see inside back cover). To lend an air of realism, I even hung a couple of fly strips, because flies would have been a curse in those days.

One thing that made this project so much easier was substantial monetary gifts from the children of the late Watson Arnold, Sr. The family also gave us several important pieces of rustic kitchen furniture. Donated in the memory of their mother, Mary Rebecca Maxwell Arnold, these pieces formed the nucleus of our kitchen collection. Many Wacoans remember the lady who just happened to have been one of the first members of Fort House committee.

In order to honor Mary Arnold's memory, we asked the local embroiderers to help create a plaque. Many thanks to Betty Clark, Dana Harrell, Aletha Keelen, Penny Lull, Lenna Vaughan, Paula Weeks, all members of the Texas Star Chapter of the Embroiderers' Guild of America. They all participated in the creation of a

delightful counted cross-stitched name plaque with Mary Arnold's full name, birth year, and death year. Set into an antique hand-carved Victorian frame, it now hangs in the breezeway just next to the kitchen.

As visitors filled Fort House Saturday afternoon, my committee and I gave tours of the house with special emphasis on the kitchen. I pointed out the marvelous faux finish on the kitchen's woodwork, window frames, and doors. All of it came from the talented hand of Doreen Ravenscroft, a former Fort House board member. Many hours of her time were donated to Fort House to accomplish this important backdrop of the room.

Another valuable contributor was house board member, Bernie Deibert, who painted walls, ceiling, and floors along with cleaning and refinishing many small artifacts. He even hung the tall black tin pipe that goes from the stove to the ceiling. Just about the time we began this project in August of 2005, I met Marge Mathias,

an avid collector of all things beautiful. Seeing our need, she began culling through her collection for appropriate pieces. She brought in flatware for the kitchen table and dozens of valuable cooking implements. Marge's most important contribution was a dear little Victorian high chair.

Many other people stepped forward to help with this project: Diana Browne, widow of collector, Lowell Browne, gave one of his handsome, earthenware crocks. Jo Ann Weaver donated the milk cooler, John and Karen Tavener of Lorena sent over a cast iron sausage press, and Linda Baker purchased the pie safe that was discovered at an antiques store in Marlin. Visitor Keith Adler was so taken with the nearly finished kitchen that he later dropped off a rustic wooden water bucket.

Claude Barron donated the use of his entertainment hall for a special fundraiser for the kitchen and Dallas Heritage Village gave us the center kitchen table. Other monetary gifts came from Dr. Charles and Jean Tolbert, Billie Brownfield, Robert Green, and surprisingly, a California friend of mine, Patti McClain.

Our kitchen is just about complete now, but it will always be a project in progress. I'll never be able to attend a garage sale or antiques store without musing about the possibility of adding a cherry pitter or an old earthenware mixing bowl.

THE GOLDEN AGE OF THE FRENCH CHAIR

In February of 2004, I was invited to deliver Historic Waco Foundation's spring lecture. This annual lecture is always the last one in the Barnes Decorative Arts course, which begins the first part of January every year.

My subject was The Golden Age of the French Chair, the 17th and 18th centuries when Louis XIV and his descendants, Louis XV and Louis XVI ruled France while residing at Versailles. These kings had little to do with actual furniture design, yet their taste certainly had an impact on its development. For practical means of identification, their names are applied to three periods.

Now, you may ask why should a person study the decorative arts? Just look around you. Our homes—even our offices to a lesser degree—are filled with decorative arts products: rugs, furniture, silver, china, glassware, and pictures on the walls. All these elements provide a graceful and attractive atmosphere to live in. Why not study the history behind them?

Some years ago, I was a guest in the home of a young woman whose big, new home was quite lavishly decorated, obviously by a professional. I spotted a large print on the wall and immediately recognized it as a picture by an 18th French court painter. "Oh, a Fragonard!" My hostess said, "What?" Suddenly, I realized the importance of "knowing" one's house and its furnishings. Right then and there, I vowed never to put anything into my home without some knowledge of its origins.

The history of furniture is inextricably entwined with history itself. When you sit in a chair with curved cabriole legs, do you know that leg shape descends from ancient Egyptian furniture? The chair itself may be English Chippendale or Louis XV style, but its legs are descendants of chairs once used by Egyptian rulers and nobles thousands of years ago.

Perhaps you have a set of Louis XVI-style dining chairs. Are you aware that their straight, fluted legs designed by 18th century French ébénists (furniture makers), were inspired by the city of Pompeii? As you may remember, Pompeii was a small Roman resort city near Naples. In AD 79, nearby Mount Vesuvius erupted, burying the city and its citizens beneath tons of hot ash. The little city slept undisturbed for the next seventeen centuries. Unearthed in 1749, the classic designs from antiquity became an absolute rage at Versailles.

Why have I chosen the French chair for my subject? I believe that we moderns are the inheritors of all these compelling historic influences. Interiors in today's decorating magazines abound with French-inspired furniture. It has never been so popular. And while contemporary furniture forms such as chests, divans, and tables have similar leg and foot styles, the chair is a perfect form to study. Quoting Catharine Oglesby from her *French Provincial Decorative Art*, she says, "A French chair has as much character and personality as any person you may know. It may be sturdy and forthright, frivolous and chatty, dignified and formal, luxurious, graceful, dramatic, inventive, reserved, humorous." She continued, "In a word, French chairs are portraits. They are all the people you know interpreted in wood and fabric far more clearly than the camera can record them. To assemble a collection of French chairs would be to create a litany of saints and sinners."

Louis XIV, the Sun King, shone the brightest of of all French kings and his name still has instant recognition. During his reign of 72 years, he encouraged French craftsmen in their creation of the finest furniture in the world. The genius of French design gave us timeless furniture forms that are still with us today.

The 17th century style, which became identified with Louis XIV was grandiose, oversized, and dignified, perfect for the vast scale of Versailles. The Louis XIV chair was an opulent, upholstered reworking of the Renaissance chair style that had traveled to France from Italy in the previous century. A Louis XIV chair always had straight legs, which are supported underneath by squared-off stretchers or a horizontal X-shaped stretcher.

In the style of Louis XIV

Upholstery consisted of *gros point* needlework, stenciled leather, cut velvet, or a large-scale brocade.

Louis XIV was succeeded by a five-year old great-grandson. This meant that his uncle, the Duc d'Orleans, had to act as a regent until the child became an adult. At the beginning of the 18th century, the previous style evolved into a more comfortable chair. The tall, straight back of Louis XIV acquired a curve at its top. The X-shaped stretcher was retained, but the straight legs were bent into that graceful curved leg previously mentioned. This transitional style, which is enjoying a great popularity today, can be seen in all the decorating magazines. It is correctly called Regence.

Regence

When we speak of the regency of France, it's important to understand that this regency was separate and apart from another regency that occurred a century later in England when George III was ill and his son ruled in his stead. It's best to use the French pronunciation of Regence for the French style, thereby avoiding any possible confusion between the two.

In the style of Louis XV

Louis XV lacked his great-grandfather's serious approach to ruling, allowing himself to be dominated by two official mistresses—Madame de Pompadour and Madame du Barry. Both women greatly influenced the decorative arts because of their insatiable appetite for beautiful surroundings. The Louis XV chair was smaller and more feminine. The nobles who lived at Versailles had grown weary of all the stiff ceremony identified with Louis XIV; they desired more intimate settings. Many of their personal quarters were rebuilt with dropped ceilings to accomplish the purpose. The curvy legs on the chair were emphasized, and the clumsy X-shaped stretcher was eliminated altogether. Upholstery fabrics evolved from the heavier velvets and brocades to a more refined *petit point* needlework or delicate flower-sprigged silk or linen.

Louis XVI was the grandson of Louis XV. The style that carries his name is identified by its straight, fluted leg carved to emulate the classical column associated with Pompeii. It is vertical and dignified. This neo-classical style was the last of the royal 18th century furniture styles.

After the French Revolution and its royal inhabitants, Louis XVI and Queen Marie Antoinette, were executed, Versailles was sacked and many of the lovely things were destroyed or sold. Business was in a turmoil at the end of the century and furniture makers well understood the need to create new furniture styles that would reflect the new government's philosophy. Any craftsman foolish enough to continue designing the neo-classical style of Louis XVI would have been in danger of the guillotine.

There was a strange period of transition at the end of the century when the noble lines of the neo-

In the style of Louis XVI

classical style of Louis XVI were given fresh ornamental motifs that were identified wtih revolutionary thought. Patriotic motifs such as crossed flags, the peasant's plow and sheaves of wheat were carved into furniture legs, which were given a new outward curvature. This brief period that lasted until Napoleon declared himself emperor in 1804 was called Directoire.

The next period of French furniture is called Empire, which would outlast by more than a decade the emperor who had influenced it. Napoleon I and his army invaded Egypt in 1799. Previously, he had conquered Greece and Italy. From then on, French furniture styles as well as architecture would be created to match the massiveness of Egypt, the grandeur of Greece, and the power of Rome. To promote Napoleon's image, furniture became massive, heavy, and masculine looking. Chairs had wooden backs and upholstered seats. Legs were heavily carved with bold military symbols such as eagles and griffons. Many chairs were given scimitar or sword-shaped legs.

The four 19th century house museums of Historic Waco Foundation have an interesting selection of French-inspired furniture. The pianos at Fort House, East Terrace, and Earle-Napier-Kinnard are graced with great, swirling cabriole legs. In the second parlor at Earle-Napier-Kinnard is a very fine example of an octagonal table with beadwork on its edges. It is four feet in diameter and has scrolled legs in the Empire style. There is a card table at McCulloch House with cabriole legs that have acanthus leaves carved on their knees. Fort House has two very fine Empire sofas, so easy to identify with their dramatic eagle wings and claw feet.

In an interview with Bruce Lipscombe, once Historic Waco Foundation curator of collections, she explained, "We see these historic styles repeated over and over through one era after another with a fresh interpretation each time. When a style is pleasing to the eye and form follows function, it will become timeless. That is what makes a classic."

GOVERNOR NEFF'S GLOBE

History and geography lovers will be interested in the handsome old globe exhibited at HWF's McCulloch House Museum. It once stood in the Texas state capitol offices of Governor Pat Neff. Since Waco was his hometown, the globe ended up here and was given to our organization by his daughter, Hallie Maude Neff Wilcox.

Globes of the world constantly change as borders are redrawn. Newly-formed countries with altered borders emerge with new names. In the far past, cartographers were always anxious to interview the valiant seamen who ventured out on uncharted waters and were fortunate enough to return to civilization to report their discoveries. A unique aspect of the Neff globe is that it shows Alaska as a territory of Czarist Russia. And therein lies a history lesson. William Henry Seward was a statesman who served on both cabinets of Abraham Lincoln and his successor, Andrew Johnson. A brilliant man with keen foresight, Seward typified the expansionist mood of 19th century United States. He always acknowledged that his most important act as Secretary of State in the postwar Johnson administration was the purchase of Alaska from Russia in 1867. Americans, who thought of Alaska as a frozen and worthless wasteland, were appalled at the $7,200,000 purchase price and laughingly dubbed it Seward's Folly or Seward's Icebox.

How could Americans have dreamed of the immense riches that would one day be discovered in that remote territory? It encompassed 586,400 square miles, an area twice the size of Texas, and had cost the United States less than two cents an acre.

Over the years with time and usage, the Neff globe has acquired a deep golden patina and there are tiny torn spots showing more than a century and a half of wear. It is 72" in circumference, resting in a 47" high wooden ebony inlaid stand. Around its equator line is a 2" wide horizontal band that shows all the signs of the zodiac.

Printed on this globe within a decorative circle is the legend: *"Cary's New Terrestrial Globe Exhibiting the Tracks of Discoveries made by Captain Cook, also that of Capt. Vancouver on the Northwest Coast of America and M.*

Delaperouse on the coast of Tartary. Together with every other improvement collected from various navigators to the present time. London. Made and sold by J. & W. Cary, Strand, March 15, 1815. With additions and corrections to 1835."

Everyone has heard of Captain James Cook, the colorful 18th century explorer and navigator. He surveyed the St. Lawrence channel and the coasts of Newfoundland and Labrador. Following Magellan's example two centuries before, he circumnavigated the earth and explored New Zealand and the coast of Eastern Australia. On another voyage, he sailed the Antarctic Ocean and touched the New Hebrides and New Caledonia. It was Cook who discovered the Sandwich Islands on a later trip where he was killed by the natives of those islands now named the Hawaiian Islands.

Cook was the first to fully grasp the need for strict dietary and hygienic ship rules that would prevent scurvy, the bane of sailors on long voyages. English sailors today are nicknamed "limeys" because Cook's ships always stocked barrels of limes, a good source of vitamin C.

James Vancouver was another 18th century English sea captain who began his career by joining Captain Cook's second voyage. Later, with a command of his own, Vancouver had orders to explore and survey the coastline of Northwest America. While on those waters, he circumnavigated a large island that was later named Vancouver Island in his honor.

The M. Delaperouse mentioned in the legend on Governor Neff's globe was a titled Frenchman, a French national hero. Otherwise known as La Perouse or Jean Francois de Galaup, he was born mid-18th century. Like so many seamen of those days, he joined the French navy at the age of 15, fought against the English, and was made captain in 1780.

In 1785, he was placed in command of two ships for an expedition to explore the west coast of the Americas. Crossing the Pacific, he explored the Northeast coasts of Asia (Tartary) and sailed through La Perouse Strait between Sakhalin and Yezo. Sensing that there might be trouble ahead, he sent a messenger from the coast of Kamchatka (near Alaska,) across Siberia to France with the precious records of the expedition. That is all that was ever heard from M. Delperouse since both ships, last seen in Botany Bay in 1788, were believed to have been wrecked north of the New Hebrides. Such is the end of many navigators and explorers.

To put the Neff globe's origin date of 1835 in perspective, the Polish composer Frederic Chopin had just met his fatal inamorata, Georges Sand, who inspired his twenty-four preludes, now counted among his finest musical compositions. In England, young Victoria had just assumed the crown of the British Empire. In the United States, President Andrew Jackson was just retiring from a long career of public service.

IF THESE WALLS COULD TALK!

It's difficult to imagine having to cope with all the household pests that were the scourge of the Victorian era, even in the finest of houses: house flies, gnats, dirt daubers, wasps, bees, ants, spiders, mice, rats, mold, mosquitoes, and weevils were just some of the threats to a housewife's domain. And she knew that every time a load of fresh peaches or a sack of flour was brought into her kitchen, there could be new invaders hidden there as well.

Housekeepers of all four of our 19th century Historic Waco Foundation houses had to battle such pests constantly. Fort House was part of a six-acre farm with fruit orchards and a vegetable garden. There must have been barns full of horses, mules, and cows. Pig pens and chicken coops would have been there, too, since we know that the Fort property provided just about all the needs of the large family and staff.

Naturally, those animals would have attracted pesky insects. In the blazing Texas summers, every window would have been open to catch the slightest breeze, so the house was vulnerable to insect invasion. Window screens weren't on the market until the late 1880s and air conditioning, a 20th century invention, wouldn't be available to central Texans for a long time.

Ants were a special form of insect invasion. You might trace a long line of black ants marching through an open kitchen window, down the wall, onto the floor and up the leg of a table to get to the sugar bowl. One way to prevent this was to set the legs of the table in little ant cups. These at Fort House are hand-crafted pottery. Each leg rests in the center with an inch of water in the little moat around the edge providing a very effective barrier. Sometimes, empty tin cans used in the same way would have sufficed.

Another enemy of the housewife was time itself. The modern convenience of refrigeration by electricity was unknown until early 20th century in Waco, as late as the 1930s for the Texas countryside. Until then, the cook had to race against the ravages of time, always trying to cook and serve meat and produce before they spoiled. Before preservatives—another 20th century innovation—sacks of flour and corn meal might harbor weevils or weevil eggs, so they would have to be sifted out before using. Milk and its byproducts, such as butter and buttermilk had to be protected from souring.

Before modern refrigerators, a milk cooler was a handy option. It is the most primitive form of food storage imaginable. Made of galvanized metal, it's just a simple set of shelves with both bottom and top made to hold a couple of inches of water. The arrangement was simplicity itself. Crocks of milk products meant for storage were set on the inner shelves. Then, a cotton bed sheet was wrapped around the entire milk cooler and pinned in place with clothespins. The sheet hung down in the water on the bottom so that the moisture could wick up in the fabric. By the process of evaporation, this wet sheet would have kept the inner shelves cool enough to delay food spoilage. A minor miracle!

Another very effective insect deterrent was fly paper. It was a long, narrow coil of paper soaked in a sticky, sweet substance that contained arsenic. Housewives hung fly paper in the kitchen in order to attract the pests, which would become stuck and die. Fly paper is still available in feed stores today.

The pie safe was a simple cabinet, many times homemade, meant for food storage. Usually, the front and side panels were made of punched tin. The punches may have been arranged in a decorative pattern, such as a Texas star. The holes were small enough to keep flies out, but large enough to permit air circulation.

Sometimes, when I look at the Fort House kitchen, I wonder what I would hear if the walls could talk. Fortunately, the modern housekeeper is spared all the labor, time, and energy that went into making a kitchen function efficiently. Keeping the fire going in the cook stove, having plenty of fresh well water on hand, washing dishes in a dry sink, baking everything from scratch, and churning butter for a large family were just some of the tasks at hand. Amidst all that back-breaking work, the cook constantly battled pest invasion and food deterioration. It couldn't have been easy.

KNIFE RESTS AND SALT CELLARS

The little glass knife rests and salt cellars seen on the Fort House dining table are replicas of important Victorian dining accessories. In those days, no properly set table would have been without them. Attractive as they are, they served a very practical purpose.

THE KNIFE REST

Barely four inches long, this length of pressed glass is meant to hold the diner's at-rest dinner knife. Knife rests have been used since possibly the 17th century. In those early days when table etiquette had yet to be refined, the diner ate with his fingers and knife and possibly, a fork. In order to prevent soiling the tablecloth, some

sort of resting place for eating utensils was necessary. During the 16th century era of Henry VIII of England, most likely it was just a piece of wood. However, during the 18th century, some designing person began to create what we now consider proper knife rests, one for each diner. On the other side of the world, China had developed chopstick rests, which served the same purpose.

Initially, a large set of rests especially designed for the master of the house existed so that he could safely rest his carving knife and fork after carving a portion of meat, arranging it on a plate, and having it delivered by a servant to a guest. Possibly, the butler would do the carving on the sideboard. Either way, the table or sideboard would need the protection of oversized rests for the carving knife and fork.

Later, in a more elaborate vein, each guest was supplied with an individual knife rest. Sometimes, they were made of porcelain to match the pattern of the dinnerware. Alternatively, they might have been made in cut glass to match the glassware on the table. Loving excess, the Victorians always took an idea to its most extreme. They made knife rests in almost any material imaginable and in almost every shape, size, and configuration possible. All metals were considered, including silver and gold, along with pottery, glass, mother-of-pearl, ivory, horn, and wood.

Knife rests made in France were called *porte-couteau*—couteau being the French word for knife. Two prominent French manufacturers of knife rests were Lalique and Gallé. In Germany, they were made under the MWF mark; in Russia, it was Fabergé. English manufacturers were Davenport, Wedgwood and Coalport.

The Victorian table must have been an absolute maze of dining accoutrements. Besides the usual knives, forks, and spoons, there were fish knives, lettuce forks, individual asparagus tongs, butter pats, knife rests, and salt cellars. A knowledgeable diner gracefully maneuvered through such table accessories, but an uninitiated guest would have been completely bewildered.

The knife rest was properly placed just above the dinner knife which, at the beginning of the meal, was set next to the right-hand side of the plate. A diner would never have begun a meal with the knife on the rest. During the meal, the knife was properly placed on the plate between bites. Only when the plate was removed between courses was the knife placed on the knife rest.

THE SALT CELLAR

From the beginning of time itself, salt has been mankind's most elemental and valued substance. Salt is a symbol that goes back to biblical times, mentioned in many contexts all throughout the Old Testament. As punishment, Lot's wife was turned to a pillar of salt. Roman soldiers were paid in salt, which gives us the origin of the word *salary*. To share salt with someone was to accept his hospitality. In ancient times, newborn babies were rubbed with salt to protect them against evil forces.

Salt is as vital for mankind's survival as water. Indeed, it is a veritable component of human life. Blood, tears, sweat, and urine all contain salt. Back to mankind's beginnings, salt has always been used to preserve and pickle food. A form of salt called natron was used in the mummification of bodies in ancient Egypt. In areas where primitive man lived inland far from the sea or lacked salt deposits under the earth, it was common for a salt-starved populace to develop goiters and other health problems.

The king always had his salt dish close at hand on the dinner table. Nobles and favored guests were seated near the king, which meant that they sat near the salt. Lower ranking guests were seated further down the table from the salt dish. A person was either "above the salt" or "below the salt," a most graphic indication of social rank.

One of history's most famous salt containers was made for Francis I of France. It was created by the high-Renaissance sculptor Benvenuto Cellini, a Florentine who had traveled to the court of this most sophisticated of kings. Worked in gold and enamel, it depicts Neptune, god of the sea, and the graceful earth goddess.

Salt dishes, originally oversized like the Cellini piece, began to be worked up as small individual dishes. During Victorian times of the Fort family, the salt dish or "cellar" would have been an important part of the table setting. The word cellar came into usage for salt dishes because as the cellar of a house was a storage place, so the cellar was a salt storage place for the dinner table.

Matching sets of cut glass knife rests and salt cellars were considered the ultimate of elegance. Today, charming Victorian conventions such as the highly collectible knife rest and salt cellar (with its own tiny salt spoon) add color and interest to the modern dinner table.

THE MAGICAL LOOKING GLASS

As a child visiting my grandmother on old Lake Waco, I always loved to play with her stereoscope, photography's first attempt at 3D. I still have it today. There is a matching wooden box filled with curved cardboard cards with a double-imaged photograph. Without their stereoscopic magic, the two pictures appeared flat, like regular snapshots. To peek at a card through the handheld gadget revealed a startling lifelike image. I could idle away an entire summer afternoon, creating my own stories about all the various picture cards that were also called stereographs.

My ever-patient grandmother never denied my sister or myself access to such marvelous things in her big, old two-story house. We were welcome to poke through all her shelves and drawers for items of possible interest. Since much of her time was spent in her gardens or directing farm workers, she was an indifferent housekeeper and never seemed to throw anything away. Her home was a child's dream come true.

But the stereoscope was not invented for use as a toy. Adults found the technology and the picture cards fascinating. Subjects ranged from exotic travel scenes to Bessie Milking the Cow. I remember that Grandmother had two stereographs that told, in sequence, the amusing story of a pretty wash maid approached by a flirtatious fellow. The second photocard shows her huffily rebuffing him only to have her skirt and lacy petticoats caught in the clothes wringer. Whoops!

The technology behind the stereoscope was developed just about the time that photography was invented in France in the mid-1830s. A stereoscope is an optical instrument that presents the viewer with two slightly differing pictures, one for each eye. The impression of depth is obtained when the brain combines the two images. The same principle is applied in binocular field glasses and binocular microscopes.

It was a British physicist, Sir Charles Wheatstone, who began constructing stereoscopes in 1838. His first images for the stereographs were drawings. In 1849, Sir David Brewster, a Scottish physicist, improved the stereoscope and invented the double camera for taking stereoscopic views. American Oliver Wendell Holmes, who would end his long life as a Justice of the U.S. Supreme Court, further developed the stereoscope that American Victorians would use.

Historic Waco Foundation has such a handheld stereoscope on display in the second parlor of Fort House Museum. It is a plain model, probably not very expensive when new. My grandmother's is quite similar. She always said she had purchased it around the turn of the century from an old peddler man.

The model at Fort House is engraved with the words: "Exposition Universelle International, 1900, H.C. White Co." It is labeled "Perfecscope, USA Pat. Office, Oct. 15, 1895, June 3, 1902, February 1, 1896."

Some stereoscopes were expensive and quite handsome. Some stood on their own stands. They all had little wire holders to clasp the stereograph that could be easily adjusted to the viewer's visual needs. Some pictures were in black and white, some in sepia or color.

The sixteen black and white stereographs for Fort House's stereoscope came in an attractive cardboard box that looks like a leather-bound book. The subject is the Holy Land with scenes of shepherds, ancient ruins, and turbaned horsemen. They are labeled Keystone View Company with offices in Pennsylvania, New York, Oregon, England, and Australia.

Up until the advent of electricity and such inventions as the phonograph and the radio, the stereoscope was a popular form of family entertainment. Today, it is an oddity, a bypassed step in the evolution of photography, the forerunner of the 3D movies of mid-20th century.

MUSICAL INSTRUMENTS IN OUR HOUSES

One of the most important furnishings of the ideal Victorian home was a musical instrument. In the days before such electrical devices as the radio and television that we enjoy today, each family provided its own entertainment.

It was quite common for at least one person in a family to play a musical instrument, so children were encouraged to practice their piano, guitar, or violin lessons. A singing voice was cultivated as well. Each of the four house museums of Historic Waco Foundation is furnished with musical instruments.

McCULLOCH HOUSE

During the Civil War when Waco University lost its piano teacher to the Confederate Army, a seventeen-year-old named Emma Bassett from Corsicana was hired to take his place. A very talented teacher, young Emma taught penmanship as well as piano to the Waco University students. Penmanship is a lost art today, but a fine hand was considered a mark of erudition and refinement in the 19th century. It was during this time that Miss Bassett met and married Champ Carter McCulloch. She continued to teach private students, as well as her own children.

A handsome rosewood piano, 1836, graces the McCulloch House front parlor. Opposite is a walnut reed or pump organ, 1904. It has the usual tall case with oval mirror and candle stands on either side.

In the older Caldwell section of the house stands an earlier portable pump organ, 1860, called a "melodeon" with ivory keys and folding lid. Such a small instrument could have been transported by wagon to camp meetings.

EAST TERRACE

This house has several musical instruments. A lovely square (strings parallel to the keys) rosewood piano, 1890, was given by Mr. and Mrs. William Hoover. It stands in the second parlor. Designed in the elaborate roccoco revival style, it has a pierced music rack and massive carved cabriole legs. The maker was Galenburg Naupel.

A golden harp, the quintessence of refinement, also stands in the second parlor. This harp is gilded with classical embellishments and was made by Lyon & Healy of Chicago, #582, manufactured under five patents. With harps, the lower the number, the earlier the instrument. It was a gift of Mrs. E. D. McCan.

Another piano with upright design, has a walnut veneer with two candle stands. The seven-octave keyboard has celluloid-covered white keys with brass handles on the sides to facilitate the moving of such a heavy piece.

A walnut reed (foot pump) organ in the western cottage style is featured in the East Terrace ballroom. Given to HWF by Mrs. Malcolm Louden, this fine instrument was manufactured in Ottawa, Ill. It features eight stops, side handles, and a great deal of carving. There is also a built-in music holder with inlay on the front.

FORT HOUSE

A fine rosewood piano, 1890, is exhibited in the front parlor. With their love of entertaining, the Forts must have enjoyed many musical evenings. Each child of that socially prominent family would have mastered some sort of an instrument and would have been expected to perform. Set in a prominent spot in the Fort front parlor, the piano has a lyre pedal, machine-worked cabriole legs, and an ornate scrolled, hinged music rack. Donated by Mr. and Mrs. Thomsen, parents of Mrs. Marshall Saunders.

In the same room is a violin and bow, 1850, with its cloth sack and leather case. It once belonged to Ferdinand Downs, brother-in-law of William Aldredge Fort, builder of Fort House. Downs brought it with him on the 1854 exodus of five hundred Alabamans to Waco just before the Civil War. Fort and his mother were part of that group. One can just imagine Downs' lively fiddle music as the folks gathered to sing and dance around the campfire each evening. Donated to HWF by Joe L. Ward, Jr.

EARLE-NAPIER-KINNARD

Both Kinnard daughters studied the piano. In Earle-Napier-Kinnard stands the only instrument original to its house. Annie Mary Kinnard's own rosewood pianoforte, 1880, is labeled "John Talmon Mfg. for Klemm & Bros., Philadelphia, Pa."

In the 1880s, young Mary was to give her recital at the Waco Female College. Dissatisfied with the piano at the college, she had her own pianoforte hauled down to the auditorium. The little lamp that she always practiced by was brought along too. Both Mary's piano and the lamp are on display today in the south parlor, along with some of her own sheet music given to HWF by the Kinnard Estate.

Arriving on the market in the early days of the 20th century, the radio brought music— popular as well as classical—to the public. We have a family story about my mother. As a wee child, she visited a neighbor who had purchased the first radio in Ladonia, Texas. She described the breathtaking new invention as being a tall cabinet with knobs. A bright yellow light beamed through a tiny aperture when the radio was operating.

Great waves of a musical concert soared out from the cabinet. Unable to grasp the intricacies of radio technology, little Emily resolved the mystery by imagining that inside the wooden cabinet, there was an orchestra of tiny men, sawing away on their tiny musical instruments!

THE NEW KITCHEN AT EAST TERRACE

It finally happened! East Terrace has just completed the furnishing of its 19th century kitchen. House members Vera Porter, Mark Arnold, and Billie Brownfield have spent several years rounding up all the necessary furnishings for this room. It's a real gem and I would urge everyone to drop by and have a look-see.

Star of the room and always the heart of a kitchen is the wood-burning, cast-iron stove. Contributed by Scarlett Holland in honor of her mother, Joyce Bowden, this authentic stove was manufactured by Andes in 1889. Its silvery filigree trim is comparable to the gingerbread trim seen on many Victorian house exteriors of the time.

Stoves such as these appear cumbersome and old-fashioned to modern eyes; but we must remember that before they were invented, the housewife had to cook her meals over a camp fire or in a fireplace. All that bending over must have been very tiresome. For the first time, the wood stove enabled the cook to work at waist level. Since there was no gauge to test its intensity, there was no way of judging the heat. The cook just popped her hand in the oven and judged whether it was time to put in the pies to bake.

The wood-burning stove came on the market mid-century, just about the same time as the treadle sewing machine. If a woman had the means to afford both of these labor-saving, expensive devices, she counted herself lucky indeed. I heard of a Clifton woman who died around the turn-of-the-century. In her obituary, it stated that she was the owner of the very first wood-burning stove in Bosque County—an indication that acquiring such a stove was an important event in her life.

During the interim of the two world wars of the 20th century, the Japanese were buying up all the scrap iron in the U.S.A. Most likely, they purchased many of these old outdated iron models, which had been replaced by gas and electric stoves. This scrap iron that the Japanese shipped home came back to us in the form of bombs and bullets. That would explain the cast iron stove's rarity today.

Another piece that would have stood in almost every kitchen of those times is a pie safe. Usually homemade, the pie safe was meant for food storage. Those small tin panels with punched holes are meant to allow for air circulation and to keep out flies and other invasive insects. Billie found it at the Scott Poage auction that was held several years ago. Bill and Lenora Parrish purchased it in Billie Brownfield's honor.

One nifty gadget that every Victorian housewife would have coveted is a lard press, sometimes called a sausage press. This handsome fixture was donated by Mrs. Arnold Mathias. A rather showy piece, this black cast-iron press is embellished in red and gilt and labeled "Enterprise Mfg. Co., Philadelphia, Pa., made in U.S.A." The ground seasoned pork or venison would be packed in the body of the press and then, when the handle was turned, the meat would be pressed down and extruded into a casing attached to the bottom hole. Voila! Sausages! Marge Mathias, a lover of rustic antiques, gave several other small kitchen appliances from her collection to this project.

Don and Mary Aileen Edwards donated a turn-of-the-century wooden ice box with the label "Knickerbocker." Owner of such a zinc-lined ice box would always leave the back door unlocked so the ice man could deliver the weekly block of ice. The ice would have been set down in the top section, cooling all the food stored in the middle section. All melted water would have drained down into a pan on the floor un-derneath. Woe to the housewife who let the water pan get too full, because then it would be spilling all over her kitchen floor.

The dry sink appears to be just a handsome little cabinet, but this is where all the dishes would have been washed. Water from an outside well would have been lugged in and heated on the stove for the chore of dishwashing. Most likely, a removable liner of metal, now missing, would have fitted down into the recessed top. It was meant to catch all dripping water from dish wash activity. This piece was given by Cindy and Brent Mattson in Billie Brownfield's honor.

The dear little homemade chair next to the dry sink speaks of days long gone. It was a gift to Historic Waco Foundation by Mrs. Paul Dickard of Colorado. This chair stood for a century in a Longview, Texas farm house kitchen. Its seat is woven cowhide, so old and worn that it's almost calcified today.

The kitchen features two butter churns, both have a vertical plunger. The earthenware churn is the type commonly used by housewives. The other is made

of wood, which would indicate a greater age. Every housewife lucky enough to own a milk cow would have churned butter several times a week.

That large wooden chest with belled-out lower drawers is called a possum belly cabinet, a handy addition to any kitchen of the past. The capacious lower drawers are lined with tin, and I would imagine that the cook would have stored her dried beans and other such dry comestibles there, root vegetables perhaps.

The East Terrace kitchen project is a work-in-progress. Dozens of small Victorian cooking implements are still needed. The basic outline of a 19th century kitchen is there in the small space at East Terrace. Much has yet to be done, though. Watson Arnold, Jr. has donated a stack of old wooden shutters, which must be cut down and installed on all the kitchen windows. Colorful dishware should be exhibited in the pie safe shelves.

The name of Billie Brownfield sparks generous attitudes in her friends. Many donations to this project in Billie's honor were monetary: Scherry Edens, Bill & Lenora Parrish, Neva Herring, Joyce Bowden, Cindy & Brent Mattson, and Marge Juren.

For 20 years, Billie Brownfield has been a faithful supporter of her beloved East Terrace, generously giving time and energy and always willing to dip into her own funds to help with various house projects. Billie is a credit to her community, a testament of what one determined person can accomplish.

TIME PIECES OF THE PAST

Scattered throughout Historic Waco Foundation's four house museums are some marvelously interesting timepieces. Ten clocks in various sizes and styles decorate mantels, desks, dressers, and shelves. Spanning a century, they date from the beginning of the l9th century into the early days of the 20th.

Let's begin with McCulloch House Museum and the tall mahogany case clock that stands in the entryway. Some people would call this a grandfather clock, but in decorative arts terms, it is correctly known as a tall case clock. It is almost twelve feet tall, made by Russelle of London in the English Georgian style, circa l800. The fancy top is called a broken scroll pediment and it's decorated with three brass finials. Other classical touches are the fluted columns with brass Doric capitals and bases.

The face of this tall case clock has Roman numerals and is highly decorated with brass. The mechanism offers two different musical chimes: the Westminster (which emulates the sound of Big Ben in London) or the Whittington. There is also a fixture that can be set to completely silence the chimes. This handsome piece came to us from the estate of Hallie Maude Neff Wilcox, daughter of Wacoan Pat Neff, one-time governor of Texas.

Another generous donor was the Pauline Breustedt estate, responsible for the gift of two handsome little l9th century mantle clocks downstairs at McCulloch House. In the front parlor is a l6" tall mantle clock with white marble columns and ormolu mounts. (Ormolu is imitation gold decoration made from an alloy of copper and zinc.) Highly decorated, it reveals tiny flower and leaf designs that are echoed in the ormolu mounts. The pendulum has the shape of a small basket of flowers. All in all, a charming piece.

Another charmer, and one of my favorites, is located on McCulloch's dining room mantle. It is fashioned in the shape of a lyre, with many floral swags and wreaths. The pendulum resembles the five strings of the lyre and around the white porcelain face with its black Arabic numerals is a circle of French paste brilliants. (French paste is a fancy term for finely worked imitation stones.)

This circle of brilliants is connected with the working mechanism, so that with every tick of the clock, the circle trembles. If the clock is set close to a window, the faceted brilliants are meant to refract the sunlight and bounce rainbows around the room.

In this case, it's especially unfortunate that this clock is not kept wound, because it would give such life to the room. Today, all the Historic Waco Foundation houses are uninhabited. The old clocks need someone around to routinely hand-wind them to keep them ticking.

A fourth clock at McCulloch is dramatically different from all the others. One of its two large faces has Roman numerals and the other large face shows Arabic numbers from one to thirty-one, allowing it to tell the date of the month. It was made by the Southern Calendar Clock Company of St. Louis, Missouri; patented March 18, 1879.

This clock sets on a little rustic homemade table with hand-turned legs. This table was crafted from the wood of a single tree and was made by Martin Patrick of Salyer, Kentucky for his bride so she would have a place to set her precious clock. The clock set atop the table all their married life and was left there by their descendants. Mr. & Mrs. William Bitner of Waco are the donors of both clock and table.

Our most feminine clock is in the upstairs bedroom at McCulloch. Standing about a foot high, its body is made of porcelain with a blue glaze and there is a romantic image of a lady and a gentleman on the front. The feet and face are decorated with ormolu and time is told in Arabic numerals. Signed "Petit, Made in France," this fanciful piece was purchased from a jeweler named Levinski, 407 Austin Ave., Waco. The Waco City Directory of 1936 lists Jacob Levinski as a watchmaker and jeweler.

We find two clocks in Fort House, both dating from about 1890. They were both donated by Mrs. Annie Turner and Miss Laura Wittcliff. In the 19th century kitchen is a two foot high German clock with Roman numerals. Inside its walnut case, there is a molded cast iron pendulum in a flower and scroll shape.

Across the river at East Terrace, there is a delightful timepiece in the family sitting room. Donated by Miss Margaret Horsfull, it dates from the 1890s. Its small size deems it perfect for setting atop a chest of drawers. The body is black metal with two ornate handles, small feet, and a white face with black Roman numerals. There are many classical decorations here: acanthus, shell, egg and dart. The label indicates it was made by Ansonia Clock Company.

At Earle-Napier-Kinnard House Museum, the visitor will spot two clocks. In the south parlor is a tiny enamel clock, circa 1900. Its white face has blue and gold floral decorations and small bronze trophies on the top. It is held up by bronze putti. (The Italian word putti is the plural for putto, which is a nude infant angel-like decorative figure seen in many works of art.) The entire piece stands on a pink marble base. The donor was Mrs. John Donnan.

Shakespeare lovers will delight at the Empire style clock in the dining room of Earle-Napier-Kinnard. It dates from 1900 and is black enamel on a cast iron base with paw feet. The face has Roman numerals, and the label reveals that it was made by Ansonia Clock Co., patented June 14, 1881, New York, U.S.A. Engraved on the back is "Judge Alexander 4, 03," most likely the original owner.

A pensive Shakespeare with quill pen in hand sits next to the clock's face amidst his manuscripts of Hamlet and Macbeth. All around him swirl classical motifs such as the anthemion, the scroll, and the sword. This was a gift of Isadore Fred who operated Fred's Jewelers, a very successful shop on Austin Avenue in mid-20th century.

As I have mentioned, all these clocks now stand silent, but there was a time when the sound of ticking and chiming clocks was very much a part of everyday life. Of course, there were other means of telling time in those days. One could simply observe the angle of the sun and have some inkling of the time. Then, there was the barnyard rooster announcing sunrise, church bells, and the noon whistle, which usually came from a factory to indicate the noon break. The dinner bell and trains that came through town at specific hours also helped tell time. Life was a bit slower in Victorian times, but a timepiece was still necessary if you were to be on time for Mrs. McCulloch's tea party.

THE STYLE OF NUMBERS

Notice that two kinds of numbers have been used on the faces of these clocks: Roman and Arabic. Roman numbers originated with ancient Rome, which existed from 500 BC to AD 500. Well into medieval times, Western Europe used the Roman numbering system.

It was the Crusades, beginning in the 11th century, that gave us Arabic numerals. Returning warriors brought them back along with all the riches of the Far East, which was then well advanced in contrast to barbarian Western Europe. Arabic numbers are probably one of the most important legacies of all five Crusades because of the Arabic zero, which greatly simplifies computation of numbers. Today, we use Arabic numbers in all our computing without even a nod of acknowledgment to their origins.

VICTORIAN WICKER FURNITURE

There is a certain airy grace about that furniture form we call wicker. Set in a Victorian parlor or a sun porch, it always appears to be welcoming to the weary visitor. By the way, do you know the origin of the word "parlor?" The French have a word for "to talk" which is 'parler'. The parlor is a room where people go to sit and talk.

At McCulloch House can be seen several pieces of 19th century wicker painted white, a popular finish. These pieces grace the upstairs front landing. With all the tall windows open on a hot summer's day to catch cool breezes from the Brazos River, the most comfortable place in the house would have been the landing. By its very lacy nature, hand-woven wicker is cool as well as comfortable.

Wicker furniture is made from the rattan plant, evoking the exotic Far East where the plant flourishes. It's easy to see why the Victorians, with their love of flamboyance, would have taken to wicker. It can be easily worked into all sorts of curlicues and fancy designs.

(Above) Roman bas relief, Bath, England
(Right) Reproduction of Roman chair

Wicker has a noble history. It was used by the Egyptians, the Greeks, and the Romans. Tomb paintings of ancient Egypt depict battle scenes where horse-drawn war chariots are shown to have wicker sides. The use of wicker meant that the chariots were lightweight and easy to maneuver. From Roman England, there survives a marble *bas relief* carved with the image of a Roman matron as she sits in a chair crafted from woven wicker. This chair (its modern reproduction is exhibited in the Bath, England Museum) has an appearance of timelessness. It wouldn't look out of place in a modern furniture showroom today.

When the Romans occupied England about 2,000 years ago, they discovered talented Glastonbury craftsmen who wove such handsome furniture from native reeds. Wicker was cheaply made, comfortable, lightweight, and therefore easy to transport. The Romans must have had wicker furniture all throughout the rooms of their homes in England.

One of the oldest wicker examples in the United States is a dainty wicker cradle exhibited in Pilgrim Hall, Plymouth, Massachusetts. Documented as having come over on the Mayflower in 1620, it was first used by the son of William White. His name was 'Peregrine,' and he was the first white child to be born in Plymouth. This perfectly preserved cradle was made in Holland where the pilgrims sojourned for a decade before they sailed across the Atlantic to their new home.

For years, shredded rattan had served as a cheap packing material for exotic Oriental imports, such as china and fine furniture. In the mid-19th century, an entrepreneur named Cyrus Wakefield brought some of this packing material home with him from the docks of Boston. Realizing its potential for furniture, he established the Wakefield Rattan Company, which opened its first factory in 1855. The company received an award for its displays of wicker at the 1876 Centennial in Philadelphia.

By 1885, Wakefield Rattan Company's illustrated catalog listed seventy-one designs for wicker rockers alone. Also listed were countless stands, divans, tea tables, library tables, bookstands, music stands, whatnots, piano seats, lounges, couches, foot stools, and ottomans.

Generally, Victorian patterns ran to the effusive. There were star patterns, sunbursts, feathers, fans, and hearts. Braiding, twisting, pleating, or winding the malleable wicker material into scroll patterns achieved further diversity. By the 1880s, the lacy-like, curlicue style was replaced by the more angular Eastlake-inspired furniture. Wicker was easily painted with popular colors such as yellow, green, red, and white. By the early 20th century, natural wicker had to compete with a modern process of winding, twisted paper treated with a glue sizing around a wire core.

FASHION

The study of fashion history has been my great love. For forty years, I have visited some of the world's great collections, always content to come home to Waco and look after our Heritage Collection. It is a great treasure trove of Waco history, each garment telling its own story and revealing its own time frame. A mere century separates these two ensembles shown at right—one from the 1860s and the other from the 1960s. The dainty little girl in corset and hoop would have lived a decidedly different life from the other in go-go boots and bold leg-revealing skirt. Even their stances are dramatically different, their fashion silhouettes emblematic of their times.

BATHING BEAUTIES

Swimwear, as we know it today, was born in the late 19th century. True, ladies of the earlier part of the century tiptoed into the water in voluminous, all-encompassing bathing dresses, but those garments only allowed the wearers to submerge themselves in the water, never to comfortably swim.

Swimwear for women at the beginning of the 20th century revealed very little since shoes and stockings were required on public beaches. Bare arms and legs were strongly discouraged. Even men had to wear swimsuits with tops. Those adventurous few who dared to challenge the law faced arrest and jail. But the tide was turning against the more conservative elements of society. By the 1920s, legs and arms were bare, and a more practical garment evolved for the serious swimmer.

Actually, swimming as a sport was rarely considered until the mid-1920s when newly-emerging swimsuit manufacturers such as Jantzen sponsored "Learn to Swim" programs in cities across the country. Suddenly, everyone wanted to learn to swim and to sport the new garment designed for that purpose. Communities across the nation, including Waco, began to build public swimming pools and indoor facilities that were known as natatoriums.

A popular Waco public pool of that era was near Alexander and 29th Street. Lena Lou Dean Staton remembers the MacArthur Swimming Pool that her father, Dr. J. J. Dean, operated during the 1920s and 30s. The pool had been built during World War I by the U.S. Army for its personnel. After the war, Dean acquired it for a commercial operation.

"All of the Dean kids enjoyed working there each summer. The water came from Waco's abundant artesian springs, sometimes so hot that it had to be cooled. My dad would order hundred pound blocks of ice to be delivered and tossed into the pool. The kids

would have a great time riding the ice blocks around the pool as they melted. We supplied grey cotton knit unisex suits with the word DEAN printed across the chest. They cost 50 cents to rent and entrance fees were 25 cents for a child and 50 cents for an adult. The pool was destroyed at the end of the 1930s," she recalled. Mrs. Staton has donated one of those grey rental swimsuits to the Heritage Collection.

Jantzen was one of the early swimsuit manufacturers. One clever early Jantzen promotional device that many of us remember was its "Red Diving Girl" emblem, a diving girl in a red swimsuit, stockings, and pompom cap. Drawn from images of divers who were training for a spot on the 1920 Olympic games team, the diving girl quickly gained national popularity.

The company made available a six-inch cast metal diving girl in two forms: a paperweight, and another with prongs to hold it atop the temperature radiator gauge of cars such as the Model T Ford. The radiator gauge became a national craze. About that same time, a two-inch cloth version was sewn on the left hip of Jantzen swimsuits. Over the years as the diving lady was modernized, her swimsuit grew sleeker and she lost her stockings and pompom cap. She disappeared from Jantzen swimsuits in the 1950s.

The 1920s saw a trend toward sunbathing, a revolutionary idea since women in previous times never exposed their complexions to the sun. "Taking the sun" replaced the earlier pastime of "taking the waters" at

chic spas and popular beaches such as the French Riviera. The sun craze quickly caught on and swimsuits grew even more revealing. Lacking commercial suntan lotions that would not be around until mid-20th century, young sunbathers used to swab themselves with a homemade solution of baby oil and iodine.

As attractive and clean-cut as the 1920 wool knit suits were, they became quite heavy when the wearer entered the water. Sometimes a wool suit could weigh up to eight pounds when wet, with a tendency to sag from the weight of the water. Manufacturers began to experiment with other materials to make their product more water-friendly.

Celebrity swimmers made media waves by always wearing the latest swimwear and promoting the new sport of swimming. Johnny Weismuller, a 1924 Olympic swimming champion, went on to a successful career in the movies as Tarzan, King of the Jungle. Gertrude Ederle, who also represented the U.S. in the 1924 Olympics, was the first woman to swim the English Channel in 1926. Another Olympic champion swimmer was the colorful Duke Kahanamoku from Hawaii where water sports have always been an integral part of its culture.

By the 1930s, womens' swimwear was showing deep armholes and low backs, a reflection of evening gown fashions of the period. At that time, experimentation with new synthetics such as rayon and latex predicted a much lighter weight garment, one that would dry quicker and fit better.

World War II in the first half of the 1940s imposed wartime shortages on America's civilian population with federal restrictions on fabric usage. To save on material, swimsuit designers invented a two-piece garment that became very popular with well-shaped women.

This two-piece garment was the forerunner of the postwar bikini, first launched in 1946 by a little known Paris designer, Louis Reard. He named his skimpy suit for the tiny South Pacific atoll of Bikini where the first experimental atomic bomb

test was conducted by the United States. This is a perfect example of current events influencing fashion.

Hollywood movies began to feature their stars in attractive swimwear. Mid-century swimming champion Esther Williams gave a boost to the industry by starring in many MGM swim extravaganzas. Her chain mail swimsuit composed of 50,000 gold flakes for Million Dollar Mermaid, choreography by Busby Berkeley, was designed by Helen Rose who used a feather-weight latex net base for the innovative garment.

With so much sunny weather and so many beaches, it's no accident that the major swimsuit manufacturers were located on the West Coast. Jantzen, which had textile mills in Seattle, led the field experimenting with innovative swimwear fabrics. In California there were Cole, Catalina, Caltex, Elizabeth Stewart, and Rose Marie Reid.

The next decade would usher in another instance of swimwear reflecting street fashions. At the very end of the 1940s, Christian Dior had introduced the New Look, a style which required waist-cinching boned corsets. Manufacturers of the 1950s such as Rose Marie Reid followed suit by producing a boned one-piece swimsuit with a very curvy silhouette, similar to that of Dior's New Look corset.

Today's swimsuit is designed for beauty, comfort, and utility with a wide range of choice. It's been a long road from the bulky, unflattering garment of a century ago. Once women saw the possibilities of modern, clean-cut swimwear and its liberating influence, they accepted it and the new sport with enthusiasm.

CHILDREN'S FASHIONS

Until modern times, children's clothing was a reflection of adult fashions. It was also an indicator of other things, such as a family's social and economic status. On the frontier where all goods were scarce and the selection was limited, an entire family might be clothed in hand-sewn garments cut from one bolt of fabric.

The Heritage Collection of HWF has many children's garments. From a lace-edged boy's suit reminiscent of Little Lord Fauntleroy to a homely gingham dress of a little girl, this collection offers special insight into the way young folks dressed in former times. *Little Lord Fauntleroy,* by the way, was the title of an immensely popular Victorian novel by Frances Hodgson Burnett. As seen in the book's illustrations, its little hero always dressed in velvet suits with ruffled lace collars and bows. This became a popular "look," and many mothers of the time dressed their little boys in lace ruffles and bows. Fashion is influenced by everything around it, and this is a good instance of fashion being influenced by a fictional character from a popular novel.

Many of the children's clothes in our collection are identified as homemade. While some were sewn with the aid of the treadle sewing machine (on the market by 1850,) many were made by hand. Only a magnifying glass will identify the tiny, evenly-spaced hand stitches and finely crafted button-holes, which so resemble machine stitching. They must have come from the nimble fingers of some long-ago mother or grandmother who lavished many hours on her undertaking.

One important item of Victorian clothing was the hat. Everyone, adults as well as children, wore some sort of head covering when they went out.

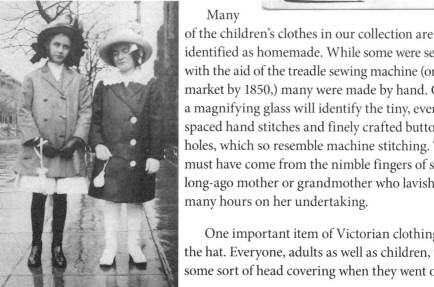

85

Girls wore hats or homemade sunbonnets. Boys wore little hats or caps. We have several fine examples of 19th century children's headgear in the Heritage Collection.

In our collection is a little boy's checked wool coat. It is decidedly homemade, most likely around the turn of the century. With its cape, it is a scaled-down version of a man's carrick coat, a popular style during the Victorian era and often worn by the coachmen of that time. This garment might possibly have been cut from a discarded adult's garment.

During the latter half of the 19th century, most boys of five or six wore pleated knee-length skirts much like the Scottish kilt. The kilted skirt was attached to a simple sleeveless bodice that was hidden by a matching jacket. After age seven or eight, boys traditionally went into knickers. By mid-teens, a boy would enter the adult world by finally donning long pants.

Today, we associate the colors pink for girls, blue for boys. But this was not always so. At a Smithsonian exhibit, I once saw a boy's 1918 white cotton sailor suit embellished with pink braid. The explanation, difficult for us to comprehend today, was that pink was considered a "stronger" color in previous times. The sailor suit has always been a classic for both boys and girls. The top with its braid-edged, square military collar and tie could be worn over a girl's skirt or a boy's pants.

Prominent personalities influence fashion. Sailor suits were sometimes called "Dewey" suits, named for Admiral Dewey, America's naval hero of the 1898 Spanish American War. Another garment in the collection that bears the name of a celebrity is a cotton print dress. The label carries the brand name of popular child movie star, Shirley Temple, and has a 1930s innovation— the zipper!

Black was a popular fashion color for children as well as women. This reflects the 19th century cult of mourning inspired by Queen Victoria's long period of widowhood. During a family's period of mourning, ideally the children would have been dressed in black garments.

The overall fashion silhouette for children during the Victorian era was influenced by corsets, another example of children's fashions mimicking adult fashions. Young boys of the mid-19th century wore corsets for posture improvement while their sisters were laced into corsets that would

mold the growing body into the desired tiny waist so necessary for wearing adult fashions.

In the HWF Heritage Collection is a tiny corset that might have been worn by an 8-year-old girl. Girls also wore crinolines and then later, the hoops of the 1860s. As women's skirts evolved into the bustle shape of the next two decades, young girls also wore modified bustles.

Today, children wear casual clothes that give little hint of social distinction. Now, girls wear pants, which would have been completely unacceptable in former times. Comfort is of paramount consideration.

Technology has always contributed to the world of fashion. Modern man-made fibers are easy to care for. The metal zipper, invented during the mid-1930s, has gone through many developments, including the plastic zipper. Velcro, from the latter part of the 20th century, is another great closure invention and can be seen today on shoes as well as clothing.

The most popular modern children's garment of all is made from denim, a humble textile originally spun for men's work clothes. The word comes from de Nîmes, meaning "of Nîmes." Nîmes is a city in Southern France, which originally produced the textile that came to be called denim. Today, blue jeans are the accepted style for young people all over the world. They may seem to be modern, but we must remember that blue jeans, made of denim in almost the same style as today, actually date back to the California gold miners of 1849. They were first made and marketed by a man named Levi Strauss in San Francisco.

Blue Eyes Mine, California, 1879.

DOWN THE AISLE IN STYLE

The Heritage Collection of HWF includes many wedding gowns from the past, each gown reflecting the taste and social standing of its owner. Each design indicates the era when it was created: voluminous skirted Victorian; leg o'mutton-sleeved 1890s; narrow-waisted and full-bosomed Edwardian; short and flat-chested 1920s; narrow and bias cut 1930s; and broad-shouldered 1940s.

Most of the gowns are white, even though many 19th century brides chose more practical colors. Perhaps there are dresses in our collection that were created for bridal purposes, but because they came with no provenance (history) and are not white, they have not been identified as bridal wear.

We have in the collection the white satin gown worn in 1887 by Wacoan Antoinette Rotan, donated by the Fentress family. By the end of the century, sleeves had begun to dominate the fashion silhouette. Known as leg o' mutton sleeves, they could be heavily padded. This bride chose voluminous sleeves to achieve the perfect silhouette of that era. Unfortunately, exhibition under harsh lighting for many years caused considerable damage to this garment. Today, we carefully follow proper museum procedures by using appropriate storage and low key lighting with limited exhibit time.

Since many brides of the past planned on wearing their bridal gowns later for special occasions, a dark color was the most practical approach. Women didn't have the extensive wardrobes that we do today, and a wedding gown would have been worn for years to come.

A perfect example of this practicality is the beautifully tailored navy blue wool suit that Mrs. Chapin Seley made for her wedding in 1910. Mrs. Seley, a Wacoan, was well known for her needle skills, and we are fortunate to have several garments in the collection from her talented hand. Studying her workmanship, I gain the impression that the diminutive Mrs. Seley was conservative in her fashion taste, but always sought to appear well-tailored with a fashionable silhouette.

One reason for choosing a colored wedding gown was a family death. Mourning in the past was generally prolonged. Rather than a black dress, a bride might have chosen from a range of colors specifically ordained for mourning purposes: purple, lavender, or gray. In the collection, we have a magenta (a cousin of purple) wedding gown from the late 19th century. We know from its provenance that it was indeed worn by a bride whose father had died while the wedding was being planned. She was Anna T. Wilson who married Samuel W. Braume in 1903. The bride's color choice may appear jarring to modern eyes, but it would have been correct mourning apparel in her day.

As a sidelight on that word 'magenta', this color is named for Magenta, a small town near Milan, Italy. In 1859 at the time of Emperor Napoleon III, the French and the Sardinians won a decisive victory over the Austrians. In those heady days of victory, Paris designer Charles Frederick Worth, always aware of publicity opportunities, created a new color. He named it magenta, a vibrant rose-purple that became the fashion rage of the 1860s on both sides of the Atlantic.

Variations on gray and purple were appropriate all through the Victorian period, which ended just about the turn of the century. In my personal collection, I have a marvelous 1860s gown that is made of royal purple silk, with that era's full-skirted, cinched waist silhouette. A California friend gave it to me many years ago. She told me that it had been worn by a Bangor, Maine ancestor who married during the Civil War. This was the second marriage for the bride who had lost her first husband to the war.

We are always excited to receive a gown accompanied by a photograph of the owner wearing that specific garment. Consider a photograph of **Ethel Mae Fanning** who married J.B. Sparks in June of 1906 in the family home at Bosqueville. Her aunt had made the lovely white gown, cut in the ideal Edwardian silhouette: high-boned collar and constricted waist.

The ideal 1920s fashion was basically a shapeless shift with little or no structure or lining. We have several wedding gowns from that decade. It's amazing to compare them with former and future styles. The 19th century gowns were constructed with great volumes of fabric. The later decades of the 1930s and 1940s also favored long skirts and trains. On the other hand, we have flapper-era wedding gowns, some of them knee-length, of lightweight silk that could be rolled up and packed in an overnight bag.

The 1930's fashion silhouette was a long, slender skirt. Paris proclaimed the bias cut skirt and fashionable women found it to be flattering. Ideally, the skirt was cut on the bias of the fabric, which assured a smooth, easy fit to the hips.

The 1940's style is exemplified by **Beverly Baine Jacobs'** white satin wedding gown, which has lightly padded shoulders and a narrow waist so popular during World War II. Beverly was the daughter of Mr. and Mrs. William Baine of Waco. She married John Jacobs and was a longtime member of Historic Waco Foundation, serving on its board for several terms. Her gown and its accompanying photograph are now part of the Heritage Collection.

It's interesting to compare the portraits of Ethel Mae Fanning Sparks, 1906, and Beverly Baine Jacobs, 1940s. Each wore the latest fashion, but the two silhouettes, four decades apart, are quite different. Each young woman reveals her personal taste as well. An undergarment always gives a decidedly different finish to the gown. Ethel Mae is tightly corseted in a full-length, boned undergarment while Beverly wears a more modern brassiere.

Both brides have long hair, but Ethel Mae has parted hers in the middle and pulled its length into a high chignon at back. Beverly wears her shoulder length hair loose with a fashionable pompadour across the front. Ethel Mae is wearing little more than a dusting of rice powder on her nose while Beverly wears lipstick, the most important cosmetic of the 1940s. Ethel Mae carries a single rose in her white-gloved hands. For her bouquet, Beverly shows a profusion of ribbons and blossoms.

THE FENTRESS FAN COLLECTION

Some years ago, the Harlon Fentress family of Waco gave 200 fans to Historic Waco Foundation. They had been collected by world-traveler Mary McLendon Fentress and were given to the organization in her name. This treasure trove of 19th and early 20th century fans—both pleated and rigid—is now housed within the Heritage Collection at HWF.

Historically, the fan can be traced back into the mists of time. The oldest use of a fan was most likely functional, a leaf pulled from a palm tree or woven from wicker. When mankind graduated from food-gatherers to food-producers, people needed to separate the chaff from the wheat and to keep the hearth fires glowing. Such primitive fans are still used in remote parts of the world, essentially unchanged from those painted in Egyptian tombs of the third millennium BC.

As the Egyptian civilization developed thousands of years ago, ceremonial fans were made with the greatest artistry and from the richest materials. The first pictorial record of a man-made fan dates from 5,000 years ago. It was a rainbow of ostrich feathers atop an eight-foot staff, a ceremonial object for the Egyptian pharaoh's court. Later, fans traveled on trading ships as they crossed the Mediterranean. The Greeks developed their own version of the fan, substituting peacock feathers for the ostrich.

A round-shaped fan with a rigid handle called the *flabellum* was developed during early Roman Christian days. For purely practical reasons, it was incorporated into the ritual of the mass, using it to protect the communion wafer from flies. As time passed, it took on a religious significance, as the priest raised it over his head at one point in the mass. The *flabellum* is no longer used, having been discontinued by Pope Paul VI in the 1960s.

The Japanese gave Europeans the folding or pleated fan, during AD 1000. It came to the West via Chinese and Portuguese merchants in the 16th century, during the Age of Discovery. The explorer Vasco de Gama is sometimes credited with introducing this little folded appliance to Europe. It quickly became the darling of fashion, remaining an important part of a woman's (and, in some cases, a gentleman's) wardrobe until early 20th century.

The first European folding fans were made in Italy in the late 16th century. An early style was called découpé. It had leaves made of pierced or cut-out paper, which was an attempt to imitate lace. It is interesting to study portraits of Queen Elizabeth of England, in which she often posed with a fan. In her Armada portrait, 1588, she carries a large ostrich fan with a rigid handle, which expresses ponderous majesty. In 1592, she is depicted holding the newly fashionable folding fan from Asia, which seems to convey a different message: statecraft combined with coquetry.

The cockade fan worked through mechanical means. We have in the Heritage Collection a marvelous Italian cockade fan made of olive wood with a mirror set into one side, circa 1850s. To open, the top tassel is pulled and the paper leaf opens and expands into a pleated circle. To close this beautifully orchestrated little mechanism, the bottom tassel is pulled and the leaf folds up and disappears into the handle.

The brisé fan was a Chinese export. The sticks (or blades) carry no separate leaves, but extend full length to provide a continuous surface for decoration, stabilized by a narrow silk ribbon running throughout the sticks. Many times, these fans were made of delicately carved, sweet-scented sandalwood.

The royal wedding of Henri II of France with Catherine de Medici of Italy introduced the fan to France in 1549. By the time of Louis XIV in the 17th century Baroque era, the center of fine fan-making had shifted from Italy to France and by the 18th century, the fan-maker's art had reached its zenith. The French encyclopedist of that century, Denis Diderot, saw that it was important enough to include an illustrated description of the many complex steps of fan-making.

Subject matter on 18th and 19th century printed or hand-painted folding fans favored fantasy or idealized subjects in pastoral or mythological settings. The French described them as fête-châmpêtre (a country picnic) or fête-galante (flirtatious dalliance between men and women.) Several of our fans depict scenes of such revelry. On the top side of the fan, you can see the gentry in fine dress. The reverse side depicts gypsies or peasants in casual or ethnic clothing. One exceptional style was the mask fan, which has cut-out eye holes through which one could spy, undetected.

Nothing epitomizes the superficiality of the court at Versailles so much as the fan. In the rarified circles of Marie Antoinette's court, an entire sign language and special etiquette developed around the fan. No one could open a fan more than half-way in her Majesty's presence. Anything that the queen happened to drop (such as a glove or a handkerchief) or that she might require, was passed to her by a lady-in-waiting on top of a half-opened fan as though it were a tiny serving tray.

Rigid 18th century French courtroom etiquette ruled out eye-glasses. Even near-sighted Louis XVI abided by this rule, thus developing an unflattering squint. The royal mistress of Louis XV, Madame du Barry, cleverly circumvented this restriction by having magnifying glasses hidden in her fans. For vanity's sake, a mirror was commonly worked into a fan guard.

Fashion is always affected by current events, and the fan industry always altered its designs to suit the times. In the 18th century French court, fans of majestic proportions balanced the excessively wide-skirted dresses. At century's end, fans

dwindled to small proportions to reflect the more slender skirts of Revolutionary times. In any case, to carry a luxurious fan from former times during the Reign of Terror, when so many aristocrats faced the guillotine, would have been unfashionable as well as politically unwise.

Held up to society, the fan mirrored it quite accurately. Fans were printed with dozens of messages, from religious sayings to fans printed with all the dates of the feast days and holidays. The great hot air balloon ascension by the Montgolfier Brothers in late 18th century France was commemorated with a printed fan. Men carried fans in the 18th century and well into the Victorian era. You can usually identify a man's fan, because there is always an insect worked into the design.

Fans were greatly influenced by the extended period of mourning after Queen Victoria lost her beloved consort, Albert. Full mourning Victorian fans were made of black silk, lace, or paper. Fans carried during the later months of mourning were painted in grey and white or mauve and white.

Fan designers knew no limits to ingenuity. Miniaturized mirrors, sewing essentials, cosmetics and grooming instruments were hidden in fan handles. Lace adapted well to fans. Whether machine or handmade, the lace was always designed and worked to the exact measurements of the fan leaf.

Surely the prize of the entire fan collection is a 14" long pleated fan, circa 1880, of Belgian bobbin duchesse lace, most likely of French origin. The sticks are made of glistening mother-of-pearl and its guard is graced with an intricately carved monogram of the lady who originally owned it. Its silk-covered box retains the paper label: "J. Duvelleroy by appointment, London and Paris."

Fans retained their popularity through the Edwardian period; however during the 1920s, the modern, emancipated woman began to smoke. Having her hands thus occupied, and perhaps no longer feeling the need for coquetry, the fashionable modern woman discarded the fan except for practical purposes. Surely, the invention of air-conditioning in the 1930s had its effect on the demise of the fan.

Some years ago, I invited a specialist to visit and document the Fentress Fan Collection. Cynthia Fendel of Dallas is a collector, lecturer, and writer on the subject of fans. She spent an entire day inspecting and dating the HWF fans. She approved of the manner of their care and pronounced the Fentress Fan Collection to be a treasure indeed.

FOR THE LOVE OF A GLOVE

More than any other article of clothing, with the exception of the hat perhaps, the glove carries special significance. How many traditions, how many sayings, center on the glove? There are many references to the glove in the English language and, more than likely, other languages as well.

"To throw down the gauntlet" originally meant a prideful, irrevocable challenge to a duel between two men that might end in death for one and possible disgrace for the survivor. Over time, to throw down the gauntlet has taken on less drastic connotations. Today, when dueling is outlawed as well as outdated, the saying has been diluted to simply mean a challenge.

One of the most touching phrases in Shakespeare's "Romeo and Juliet" refers to a glove. How many love-struck Romeos over the last four hundred years have uttered these sublimely beautiful lines from the stage? "Would that I were a glove upon that hand, that I might touch that cheek."

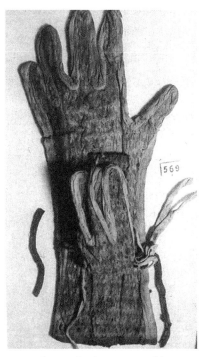

From the beginning of recorded history, the glove took on a symbolism of its own, no matter the country. An ancient Chinese custom focused on hospitality. When a guest entered a home, he was immediately given a leather glove as a symbol of warm welcome. If the gesture were withheld, it indicated that the person was not welcome.

From the tomb paintings of Egyptian pharaohs, we have proof of the existence of gloves more than 3,000 years ago. In 1923, when the tomb of King Tutankhamen was opened, several pairs of gloves were found. They appeared to have been made of tapestry-woven linen. Since the sun-beaten desert of Egypt would not have required weather-protective clothing, the young king may have worn such gloves for chariot driving or hunting. Perhaps they were used for ceremonial purposes.

From the tomb of King Tutankhamen

Long before the Christian era, in the process of a sale of land, a glove was given to the purchaser as a guarantee that the title and deed were authentic. Glove-barter

95

during the Middle Ages was an act of "throwing down the glove" wherein a peddler would toss down a glove as evidence of his honesty in trading. Well into the 20th century, in the public markets in England, a courier proceeded through the area carrying a glove mounted on a tall staff to proclaim the opening of honest trading.

In the early days of glove-making, gloves were rare and most difficult to obtain. Just consider the dozens of little segments of leather or fabric that have to be pieced together to create a supple, comfortable covering for the hand with its five fingers. A glove has to fit well, yet be flexible enough for the wearer's hand to function.

In the far past, a young man gave his father-in-law a pair of gloves as a symbolic guarantee that he would be responsible for his bride. Because of their value, a gift of gloves was just as binding as an engagement ring, for both the giver and the recipient.

The use of funeral gloves goes back many hundreds of years when high-ranking persons were buried wearing their gloves. In 1738, Governor Belcher of Massachusetts provided more than one thousand gloves to be worn by all mourners at his wife's burial services. Up until the end of the 20th century, most morticians provided white cotton gloves to each pall bearer at a funeral.

In early Christian days, because gloves were so closely associated with celibate churchmen, women were forbidden to wear them. Perhaps women wore the lowly mitten in cold weather, along with the lower classes. There is an early mention of King Henry IV of England, who permitted glove makers to sell hawking gloves for ladies. The hawking glove was a gauntlet with a wide cuff, which protected the wearer from the claws of the falcon that perched on her wrist while pursuing the ancient sport. Slowly, the glove was accepted as proper fashion accessory for women. Fashion-conscious Catherine de Medici, who married Henri II of 16th century France, set the trend of women wearing gloves at court.

Gloves have always been synonymous with royalty. They represented the power and authority of the kingdom. As a king lay dying, he would ceremoniously hand his gloves to his son or the next in line to rule. Henry VIII of England, who ruled with an iron fist, is often portrayed with gloves in hand or tucked into his belt. The British Museum exhibits one of his gloves of chain mail and leather, so constructed that when his gloved hand was closed around a sword, it could not be wrestled from his hand in battle.

The glove reached its height of sumptuousness in the 16th and 17th centuries. Inordinately fond of beautiful clothes, Elizabeth I of England is reputed to have owned more than two thousand pairs of gloves at her death. In the museum at Saffron, England, a single embroidered glove is exhibited, said to have belonged to

Mary, Queen of Scots, Elizabeth's nemesis. The doomed woman supposedly removed her gloves as she walked to her execution, giving the precious things to her favorite lady-in-waiting as a keepsake.

In the 18th century, it became popular to use the back of leather gloves to display a printed message. Later in 1825, when the elderly Marquis de Lafayette visited

18th century printed leather glove

the United States, women in every city that he toured wore white kid gloves especially made for the occasion. They were printed with Lafayette's image. As the Marquis bent over each lady's gloved hand, he was amused to see that he was kissing his own image.

Into the 19th century, gloves became a required accessory for well-dressed men and women. A lady never ventured onto the street without being properly gloved. There is a very telling scene in a short story by Edith Wharton about a French lady, who breathlessly rushes to meet her lover. In her haste, she walks out her front door gloveless. Realizing her faux-pas, she quickly dons and buttons the gloves before finally venturing into the public eye.

During mid-20th century, shopping for a new pair of fine leather gloves could almost become a ceremony. I remember at Goldstein-Migel's, a lady could sit down in the glove department and fit her elbow into a little velvet doughnut on the counter. With the arm in this stable vertical position, the clerk might have spent an hour or so tugging on various styles and sizes to finally please the customer.

Gloves, along with the hat, were a vital part of the fashion silhouette until the mid-20th century. Then, as hats began to disappear in the 1960s, gloves followed suit. An entire industry disappeared and today, just about the only gloves that are worn are for protective purposes, such as industrial, driving, gardening, or winter sports.

THE HAT: ITS HEYDAY AND ITS DEMISE

In Edwardian times when large hats abounded, it was the custom to discreetly hand a little card to a lady in the audience of a theater. It was printed with the request, PLEASE REMOVE YOUR HAT. We have one of these little cards in the Heritage Collection.

Whatever happened to the hat? There are several reasons why head-gear has fallen to a secondary or even non-existent role on the high fashion scene.

Since hats and hairdos are closely associated, it's especially ironic that the hair stylists of the 1960s were responsible for the hat's demise. Their heavily-lacquered bouffant and beehive hairdos presented no resting place for a hat.

First Lady Jackie Kennedy, who was chic to the core and most assuredly a fashion leader, never really liked to wear hats. But she dutifully wore negligible little pillboxes at the back of her head. By affecting such simple styles, she unwittingly encouraged an atmosphere free of hats.

Three young women in Edwardian regalia

If all that weren't enough, even the Pope became involved in the controversy. In 1962, the Catholic Church, under Pope John XXIII, began a world-wide meeting in Rome called Vatican II. Among its many decisions was one that abolished the centuries' old tradition of women having to cover their heads while in church.

The result of all these influences was that women lost the habit of the hat. Milliners in every country were suddenly out of work. Ancillary manufacturers who supplied the needs of the milliners for such goods as ribbons, feathers, veiling, fabric flowers, straw and felt shapes closed their businesses. Because gloves always accompanied the hat, they were no longer worn by bare-headed women. U.S. glove manufacturers, employing thousands of highly specialized craftsmen, closed shop forever.

But there was a time when a hat was the final topper, the exclamation point to every costume. It was a means for a woman to make her strongest, most personal, fashion statement: flamboyant, eccentric, romantic, demure, or briskly tailored.

A woman could even hide beneath her hat. A timorous sort could don a sweeping, dramatic wide-brimmed hat and think of herself as a romantic heroine. A strong willed woman could hide her aggression behind a demure flower-trimmed bonnet.

Watching old 1940s movies reveals a clear statement of fashions of those days. A lady never left the house without her hat and gloves. Men always wore hats too, removing them when entering a house and donning them again when leaving. There is an old photograph of Austin Avenue, circa 1900, where every single person, man or woman, is wearing some sort of headgear. The street seems to be a sea of hats. Even little boys sport caps or straw hats.

Edwardian hats may have been large, but not all were particularly attractive.

Speaking of men's hats, another lost social custom is the tipping of a hat. It was a gallant salute to a lady that she acknowledged with a prim smile and a nod of her head. When approaching a man friend, a gentleman would touch the brim of his hat as a friendly greeting. Men always politely removed their hats in elevators, especially in the presence of a lady.

Centuries ago, hats were even more important than in modern times. In Renaissance Florence, for example, custom obliged each citizen to wear some sort of headgear, instantly recognizable according to rank, sex, and occupation. A university scholar would wear a velvet mortar, a lowly carpenter a leather skullcap. A Medici princess might choose a jeweled turban, her servant girl a simple homespun cap. Everyone knew his or her place in that class-conscious society and dressed accordingly.

99

This may be another reason that hats are worn so seldom today. Our country's egalitarian attitudes discourage such class distinctions. Rich or poor, young or old, Americans have grown used to wearing casual attire such as blue jeans, which don't require headgear. This has contributed further to the blurring of social distinctions and a more casual attitude toward the rules of etiquette.

The heyday of the hat in this century was the Edwardian period, from 1900 to about 1915. Women wore enormous cartwheels trimmed with every conceivable material such as ribbon, flowers, feathers, even entire birds. Egret feathers were especially popular. This beautifully plumed bird was almost hunted to extinction, a crisis that led to special protective legislation.

To create a base for such tea tray-sized hats, the Edwardian woman cultivated long hair, pushing it into grand pompadour hairdos. Six to eight hatpins were required to anchor

Edwardian excess, designed in Paris.

the hat to these confections. Hat pins of that era grew so long that many cities passed ordinances requiring screw-on tips to protect the eyes of streetcar patrons.

In a most dramatic turn-about, the 1920s short hair craze for women left nothing upon which to anchor hats from the previous decade. The entire silhouette changed from the corseted, modest Edwardian style to a shorter, boyish, more emancipated silhouette. American women had received the vote by 1920. Surely

this must have dramatically changed the way women perceived themselves. Short hair in the 1920s was symbolic of womens' emancipation.

The 1920s cloche, fitting as tight as a helmet over short hair, would have rendered obsolete the PLEASE REMOVE YOUR HAT card of previous times. Hundreds of thousands of such cards must have been printed and handed out by the theaters. Somehow, this card survived to give us insight into a small area of fashion history.

1920s silk brocade cloche

MY HAT COLLECTION

My special interest in hats began years ago when I lived in the San Francisco Bay Area. I had been studying fashion history in college and quite naturally, began to collect antique clothing and accessories. It was the fashion accessories that really touched my fancy, especially hats from the first half of the 20th century. Amassing dozens of outstanding examples of millinery and all their time-appropriate accessories such as purses, furs, jewelry and gloves, I began giving hat show programs for women's groups of the Bay Area.

The first hat in my collection—1940s silk organza picture hat topped with cabbage roses.

This is the very first hat in my collection, dated 1940s, found in a Pasadena, California antiques shop. This gorgeous picture hat is labeled *Bullock's Wilshire* (very posh shop on Wilshire Boulevard in Los Angeles) and most likely cost several hundred dollars when new. It is made of silk organza over a wire frame and the brim is decorated with large silk cabbage roses. What woman wouldn't feel like a queen in such a hat?

Folks seldom wear hats today, but in the past, they were practically mandatory. Worn at the very top of the fashion silhouette, the hat proclaimed a person's place in society. People ask me about the disappearance of the hat. We Americans live in an egalitarian society where a person's social or occupational identity is unimportant, so we have evolved to a point where headgear as a means of identification is deemed unnecessary. I'm also convinced that the blue jean revolution is a factor, since such a casual silhouette needs no topper.

Old movies from the early 20th century are always an exercise in the use of a hat. The leading man goes out and he puts on his hat. He comes back in and removes his hat. Ladies were always properly hatted and gloved, since the two traditionally went together. Of course, in a social situation such as a tea party or a church gathering, she would not remove her hat. Most likely, she would not remove her gloves, either.

There's an amusing story about New Yorker Bella Abzug, one of the few women to be elected to Congress in the 1960s. In her campaigning, she always wore a hat, making it her trademark. On her very first day at Congress as she entered the hall wearing a hat, one of the porters asked if she would be removing it in the manner of all the other congressmen. Of course, he most likely had been put up to the joke. She rebuffed him and sailed on into the great hall to take her place, still wearing her hat.

Today's serious collector is usually interested in hats dating no later than the 1950s. I believe the most distinctive hats date from the Edwardian period (1900-1915) to the WW II years of the 1940s. Edwardian milliners showed little restraint when it came to daring shapes and embellishments. They created hats as wide as tea trays and piled them high with feathers, flowers, and an occasional stuffed bird. This reminds me of fashion's most daring fashion designer of mid-20th century, Elsa Schiaparelli. Claiming that women would wear the most outrageous headgear, Elsa bragged that she could make a hat out of anything. On a dare, she chose the shape of a shoe, fashioned it out of felt and plunked it on a model's head. LIFE magazine ran a full-page photo of the crazy style.

Here are other hats from my collection. This provocative little straw pillbox with a silk scarf, 1940s, was the ultimate in flattery. The sales woman would have cooed, "My dear, it's you!" It was made during WW II when the fashion silhouette featured padded shoulders and short skirts. Wartime textile shortages had brought about government restrictions, which regulated the amount of fabric that could be used for a garment. Perhaps because of these restrictions on clothing, milliners had a field day and their imaginations knew no bounds.

The ultimate in sophistication is this tiny straw circle with a medieval-style silk drape, 1940s.

My husband laughs every time he sees this checked wool number, circa 1940. He's convinced that the milliner was influenced by the swirling, modern rooftop of the General Electric building at the 1939 World's Fair in New York. As a little boy, he had attended the fair, which was called The World of Tomorrow. All the pavillions were very dramatic and futuristic. This hat was custom made to match a checked wool coat, which unfortunately has disappeared.

This sweeping wide-brimmed 1910 number was custom made for a prominent Berkeley, California woman named Mrs. Edith Tibbetts. Years ago, when she cleared out her grandmother's three-story Maybeck home, her granddaughter gave me Mrs. Tibbetts' entire wardrobe, including twenty custom made hats. Even though I have purchased many vintage hats at estate sales and antiques stores, my very best numbers have been given to me by friends.

In the past, I have given dozens of hat shows here in central Texas, from Temple to Fort Worth. In the manner of the great days of the French milliners, my models always wear simple black dresses. The hats are always highlighted and shown with period-appropriate accessories. I've produced at least seven hat shows here in Waco, usually as fundraisers for Historic Waco Foundation. My last show in June of 2011 at Barron's on Fifth benefitted Fort House Museum.

LADIES IN WAITING

It was a common condition though seldom acknowledged by its real name. The average Victorian married woman might experience it a dozen times in her lifetime. Charles Dickens' wife endured it ten times. Some Victorian women considered it "the valley of the shadow of death" and purposely chose lonely spinsterhood instead of marriage.

"Expecting," "In a family way," "Her delicate condition," "With child," and "Wearing a shawl," always uttered in whispered tones, were some of the quaint euphemisms coined in those less enlightened, puritanical times. Queen Victoria, who had nine living children, detested the entire nine-month state, referring to it in a letter to her grown daughter who just happened to be undergoing the same condition at the same time as, "I'm in for it again."

Today, it seems strange to us that so common a condition, one upon which humankind's very existence hinges, should have been described in such prim, hooded language. Yet, it is only within the last few decades that polite society finds it acceptable to call pregnancy by its real name.

This would explain the scarcity of written history of maternity clothing as well as the absence of photographs of expectant women. It's incongruous that there is so little mention of such clothing in fashion history books when obviously it was so commonly used by every class of society. To study women's diaries and journals, you will never see the written word "pregnant." Even in these most intimate forms of expressing their thoughts, women only slantingly refer to some sort of lingering illness.

Popular turn-of-the-century mail order houses such as Sears Roebuck sold nursing corsets, 85 cents, but no dresses expressly designed for those months of gradual waist expansion. The only appropriate garment shown is a wrapper, although the accompanying descriptive text never mentions the word, "maternity."

According to Heather Palmer, Curator of Woodlawn Plantation in Mount Vernon, Virginia, the loose-fitting wrapper was a popular garment for housework and was sometimes called a "mother hubbard." To the modern collector, the difference between the two is minimal. Wrappers are most often seen in Eastern collections and are made of materials other than humble calico, such as silk or wool.

Curator Palmer's prodigious research into the subject of maternity was gleaned from dozens of diaries and letters of 18th and 19th century women. She has found that mother hubbards or wrappers may have been used for maternity purposes, but never entirely took the place of specific maternity dresses. Even in a rural society on the frontier, most women had maternity garments which were worn again and again, and were often lent back and forth between friends and family members who found themselves "in the family way."

A good example of this custom of borrowing is the black sateen wrapper, circa 1880, in the HWF Heritage Collection. It's signed in ink on the inside yoke, "Mrs. J.T. Mahan." The fashion historian can only speculate, but this very likely indicated that the lady might have lent it to expectant friends or relatives. I would surmise that her signature was a means of ensuring its return after so many months of wear by the borrower.

The 1897 Sears Roebuck catalog shows wrappers ranging from 85 cents to $1.75, also available in grey calico for "half mourning," 69 cents. Mrs. Mahan's black sateen wrapper would have been appropriate for "deep mourning," and a grey garment appropriate for "half mourning," a term used for the later months of mourning.

Paul Poiret, 1922

We often read that Victorian and Edwardian women chose seclusion during their expectant months since the swollen figure was considered an embarrassment best hidden away. Obviously, the shame of pregnancy stemmed from its unmentionable source.

Seclusion may have been the ideal, yet many a working class woman must have had to toil in a factory, mill, or on a farm right up to the end of her term. Her economic situation would have precluded the luxury of restful seclusion. Mrs. Theodore (Edith) Roosevelt wrote in her diary of an outdoor hike with her family when she was nine months pregnant around the turn of the century. The First Lady couldn't have been too embarrassed by her condition.

Among the fascinating discoveries of Curator Palmer's research are the survival statistics of pregnant slave women versus those of white women in pre-Civil War times. Slave women, especially on the larger plantations, were traditionally given restful retirement from kitchen or field work during their last months of pregnancy. They and their babies had a higher life expectancy than working class white women who would have worked until they delivered. The reason was purely economic. A slave might be able to give birth to several more children in her lifetime. She and her babies had a commercial value. White women were replaceable since they had no such value.

Far at the other end of the spectrum was Mrs. Edith Tibbetts of Berkeley, California, who had earned two degrees from the University of California at the turn of the century: a degree in agronomy and a degree in musicology. She was a wealthy, sophisticated woman who had her baby in 1906. The date can be pinpointed because 1906 was the year of the Great San Francisco earthquake.

We know from her granddaughter, who gave me the dress, that this Alice blue, empire-waisted garment was designed especially for Mrs. Tibbetts' pregnancy. Surely, her husband wasn't the only person present at her dinner table when she wore such a stunning garment with a long train. Since she was an avid dévotée of the opera, I can just imagine her appearing at the annual opening of the San Francisco opera in this gown accessorized with long evening gloves and a fur.

We know that Mrs. Tibbetts was in labor during the '06 earthquake. Fearing that the building was unsafe, hospital workers

Mrs. Tibbetts' 1906 opera gown

moved her and other patients to the nearby open space of Golden Gate Park. Mrs. Tibbetts lived, but her baby did not survive the ordeal.

By the liberated 1920s, the old taboos were fast fading away. American women had received the right to vote, which would naturally have encouraged them to take a more sensible approach to life. In any case, the fashion world had taken a radical turn from ankle-length, corseted garments to shorter, less restrictive styles. Maternity wear followed the general trend.

As early as 1911, a small handbook called *Children's & Maternity Garments*, published by Women's Institute of Domestic Arts & Sciences, Scranton, PA, showed illustrations of good-looking maternity styles from Butterick, McCall, and Simplicity pattern books for the home seamstress.

One of the most successful pioneers in maternity clothing was a Texas-based firm. In 1941, a Dallas woman named Elsie Frankfurt and her two sisters began to manufacture under the name of "Page Boy." Beginning with a mere start-up of $250, they made their first million dollars by 1955. The Page Boy innovation was a stretch panel set into the front of the skirt, which accommodated the bulging figure. This panel was hidden under a matching loose box jacket. Comfortable, reasonably priced, and attractive, the Page Boy silhouette had great success all across America for several decades.

An exhibit of maternity wear that I created years ago, Ladies in Waiting, sought to illustrate the evolution of maternity wear, from the 1880 homemade wrapper which shrouds the entire body to a figure-revealing, two-piece commercially produced 1960s silk dress. Today, pregnancy is considered a natural state and modern maternity fashions reflect these enlightened attitudes.

THE LITTLE TRAIN THAT COULD

Sometimes, the smallest thing can evoke a memory in the most uncanny way. In the Heritage Collection of Historic Waco Foundation, there are two small buttons that have long intrigued me.

They are identical round buttons made of a coppery-brass material, about ¾ of an inch in diameter. Across their front is the image of a streetcar with the words: Interurban Special. They must have come from a uniform of a motorman or conductor of the early 20th century Central Texas mode of public transportation, the Interurban that so many of us remember.

The Interurban always seemed like the brave little train in my childhood storybook entitled *The Little Engine That Could*. I remember that the Interurban's tracks ran on the eastern side of the highway between Dallas and Waco, parallel with the tracks of the Missouri, Kansas, and Texas railroad. When our car passed the Interurban, we children always knew that the friendly motorman on the perky little train would return our waves across the intervening cornfields.

The Interurban was a friendly mode of transportation that began in 1913 and ran successfully until the Texas Electric Railway Company discontinued service in 1948. It was also a safe ride. My parents used to put my baby sister and me on the Interurban in Dallas and my grandmother would fetch us at the Waco station. It was a grownup adventure to travel alone at that tender age, and I always knew that the conductor would see that we were safely delivered to my grandmother.

Many people remember the Interurban as a slow, bumpy ride, but I always relished the electric wires singing overhead and the wind in my face through the open window as we sailed through the countryside. Sometimes, the train would tootle along at the speed of 65 mph, faster than our father's Packard sedan could travel on the crowded two-lane Dallas highway.

Actually, Interurban cars were identical to the single streetcars seen on Waco streets, but on Saturdays and Sundays two cars were joined together in order to handle the increased traffic. During school, this handy means of transportation was popular with students. For years, the Interurban enjoyed an almost complete monopoly on passenger traffic between Dallas and Waco. Charging $2.40 for the complete trip, it offered frequent service and many stops.

The limited runs took about three hours from Dallas to Waco—stopping at larger towns such as West, Abbott, Hillsboro, Italy, Waxahachie, and Lancaster. The local run was about four and half hours as it stopped at dozens of small country towns. It would even stop for a farmer who stood by the tracks and signaled for a ride.

In addition to the Dallas-Waco route, the line was extended from Dallas to Corsicana and from Dallas to Denison up near the Oklahoma border. Once Highway 35 was widened during the 1940s to accommodate ever-increasing motor traffic, the passenger count fell drastically and the Interurban Company closed down.

Following the same schedule of the electric cars, Waco public transportation was then supplied by buses of the Texas Electric Bus Company. The car barns at Washington and Fourth Street were converted into a terminal for the new city buses.

The fifty-five outdated, but still sturdy, Interurban cars were sold to be used as shelters at camp and picnic grounds around the countryside. The rails were taken up, the scrap metal sold, and "the little engine that could" disappeared from the Texas landscape forever.

Postcard from the collection of Agnes Warren Barnes

MAUVE: THE COLOR THAT CHANGED THE WORLD

In 2002, I created an exhibit that featured mauve, the color that changed the world. Several garments from the Heritage Collection were exhibited. All sorts of shades of lavender prevailed there. It was a color that had reached the heights of popularity during the mid-19th century. The story of mauve and its creator reads like a romance novel, rich with coincidence and flamboyant personalities. Indeed, mauve would be prominently mentioned in literature including the well known works of fiction set in Victorian times: Oscar Wilde's *The Portrait of Dorian Gray,* 1891, and John Fowles' *The French Lieutenant's Woman,* 1969.

Around 1857, a fad for a new color began to flourish in Paris, the capital of the fashion world. It would travel throughout all Europe and the United States. The magical color was mauve, the French name for the mallow plant which has lavender-colored flowers.

Up until mid-19th century, dyes were made from plant and animal sources. For instance, purple came from the murex, a tiny sea mollusk that had been harvested by Mediterranean people for more than 3,000 years. Pliney the Elder, AD 77, described the technique of making purple dye in his *Natural History.* Thousands of murex, prevalent in tropical waters, were crushed and boiled to make royal Tyrian purple dye which came to symbolize sovereignty and was used exclusively to tint the robes of the Caesars.

A Mexican cactus insect was introduced into 16th century Europe by the returning Spanish conquistadores. Called cochineal, it produced a scarlet shade. Madder (red) and indigo (blue) were two very popular common vegetable dye sources. Other plant dyes were saffron, brazilwood, turmeric, and woad (a plant that gives up a blue dye from its leaves.) Until mid-19th century, the world was limited to the very narrow range of primary colors of red, blue, and yellow along with brown and black.

Appropriately, it was a woman who gave impetus to the popularity of the new color. Eugenie, wife of Emperor Napoléon III of France, decided that mauve matched her eyes. With Empress Eugenie's fashion authority, extravagant taste, and unlimited budget, she set the stage for a petticoat revolution.

Because of her influence, her friend Queen Victoria wore a gown of rich mauve velvet when her daughter married Prince Frederick William of Germany in 1858.

Later in the century in far off Russia, Czarina Alexandra discovered the color and had her boudoir swathed entirely in mauve. Everyone just had to have a lavender dress, hat, gloves, purse, fan, etc. It was a craze that swept the fashion world and made its inventor rich.

His name was **William Perkin** (1838-1907), a young Londoner from a middle class background. A gifted student with a natural curiosity for the world about him, Perkin initially showed an interest in music, photography, engineering, and painting. But it was the subject of chemistry that finally claimed his full attention. William Perkin's discovery of coal tar dyes would change the way that people see the world forever. Just think, almost everything outside of nature itself is touched by dye in some way or other. A world without dye would be a dull place indeed.

When Perkin was thirteen, his wealthy father enrolled him in the City of London School, not far from St. Paul's Cathedral. Fortunately, it was one of the few schools in the country to offer lessons in chemistry, a subject which had little practical use at the time. Thomas Hall was the chemistry instructor there and Perkin would always acknowledge his debt to Hall. Later, Perkin would attend lectures at the Royal Institution where he was the youngest spectator. In 1853 when he was fifteen, he enrolled at the Royal College, directed by the brilliant German chemist August Hofmann.

Since the study of modern chemistry was still in its infancy and a career as a chemist would be doubtful, the elder Perkin objected at first, but he was an indulgent father and he finally relented after several conversations with Thomas Hall. Within five years, William Perkin had made his fortune.

Experimenting in his laboratory, Perkin searched for an artificial means of reproducing quinine. Natural quinine, made from cinchona bark, was expensive and in limited supply. This was at a time when "the sun never set on the British Empire" and malaria was a blight on the lives of Englishmen stationed in India, Africa, and other tropical British colonies.

Actually, malaria could even be found close at home in the boggy marshes of Essex and Cambridgeshire. In his 19th century English novel, *Great Expectations,* Charles Dickens describes the notorious malarial marshes of Kent.

Laboratory experiments sometimes produce the most unexpected results. William Perkin never solved the quinine problem, but his tinkering with coal tar produced a strange mauve-colored liquid. Most single-minded chemists would have tossed out the failed experiment and begun again, giving no thought to its possible application as a dye for women's clothes. Young Perkin experimented further, stained some silk with the liquid, and quickly recognized its possibilities as a commercial dye.

The world of chemistry was given a great boost when the farsighted Albert, prince consort to Queen Victoria, directed the Crystal Palace Great Exhibition in London's Hyde Park in 1851. Highlighting modern industrial developments to thousands of visitors from all over the world, it also featured William Perkin and his discoveries.

Even though William Perkin, a modest and unaggressive man, was able to garner immense profits from his initial discovery of aniline coal tar dyes, it was impossible to completely protect his patent interests, especially when the English government lacked the vision to help protect those interests. The Perkin factory was constantly visited by French and German chemists who took his ideas back home to their burgeoning dye industries, a case of Victorian industrial espionage. Germany would ultimately dominate the world market in dyes, much to England's regret in later years.

Perkin's humble coal tar derivative would dramatically change the world of fashion and chemistry forever. While he gave the world an entire new rainbow of colors, he also opened up the field of future chemistry experimentation in other fields such as medicine, perfumes, food additives, explosives, photography, and plastics.

THE MECHANICAL HAT OF DR. McGLASSON

O ne of the most fascinating donations to the Heritage Collection of Historic Waco Foundation is a silk opera hat. It was given to us several years ago by Claude Barron and was once worn by his great-uncle, Dr. Irvy Lee McGlasson of Waco, one of Texas' most prominent skin specialists of the 19th century.

Having graduated from Kentucky School of Medicine in 1896, Dr. McGlasson became renowned for his expertise in this special field of medicine. Just after graduation, he married Della Alice Barron, daughter of a prominent early Texas family in the Axtell-Elk area, east of Waco. Beginning his medical practice in Elk, he became quite active in the Masonic Lodge there. His interest in the Masons extended into the rest of his life.

McGlasson maintained offices in three cities, practicing during the year four months each in Galveston, San Antonio, and Waco, where he had a two-floor office in the Amicable Building. Whenever he traveled to Galveston or San Antonio to work, he would go by train accompanied by his Lincoln car traveling on a railroad flat car. In 1909, Dr. McGlasson presided as Chief Parade Marshal in the very first Thanksgiving Baylor Homecoming Parade, which included 66 decorated automobiles.

Off to an adventure in the tropics in 1914, Dr. McGlasson served as chief medical officer during the building of the Panama Canal. He would go on to pioneer the use of radium and in 1924, was asked to hold a scientific program for the use of radium in the treatment of sarcoma. Dr. McGlasson passed away in 1926 at his home at 1715 North Fifth Street (which once stood between Barron's on Fifth and Earle Harrison House.) Among his many scrapbooks and clippings are dozens of calling cards sent with flowers to his funeral.

The label on the satin lining of Dr. McGlasson's top hat reads: "C.H. Gwythe & Son, 13 Holles St., London, imported by Robt. Cohen, in Galveston, Texas, U.S.A." With its exaggerated height of crown and snappy brim, the glamorous top hat was always an exclamation point to a gentleman's evening suit. This type of top hat is called a Gibus, the name of the Frenchman who invented it in 1832 and patented it in 1837.

It was designed to be carried flat under the arm and with the slightest tap, the collapsed hat would pop open. It seems as though the top hat took too much space in the opera house cloak room, so Monsieur Gibus designed an interior mechanical device. Folded down flat, a top hat could be set on a shelf at the opera house cloak room, thereby requiring a minimum amount of space. Hence, it's general name, the opera hat.

Dr. McGlasson must have given this dashing headgear a great deal of use since today it appears to be well worn. It has been sent off to a conservator who restored the inside mechanism to its original pristine condition. A tip of the hat to Claude Barron, who so generously funded the restoration of his great-uncle's century-old top hat and gave it to the Heritage Collection of Historic Waco Foundation.

Along with this collapsible top hat, Claude Barron donated Dr. McGlasson's black wool three-piece evening suit, circa 1920, which consists of a top coat, vest, and pants. The coat's label reveals a local origin: "Shaffer & Duke, Waco, Texas." There are signs of wear, yet all three pieces appear to be in good shape, considering their age.

Another top hat can be found upstairs in the ballroom at East Terrace House Museum. Set under the protective covering of a Lucite box, it is safe from dust and excessive handling. Actually, just to touch this hat would be dangerous since it's made of beaver felt, a material that was processed in a mercury bath.

Victorian hatters would work up to their armpits unprotected from these harmful chemicals, unaware of the danger. When Alice in Wonderland speaks of the Mad Hatter, she is alluding to the fact that during the 19th century, a hatter would have lost his mind after a career of working bare-armed in highly toxic mercury compounds. Today, museum curators know that they should steer clear of such artifacts, since they are still dangerous to the touch, even after a century.

THE PIONEER SUNBONNET

One of the most important garments for a pioneer woman was a deep-brimmed bonnet. Developed as a practical solution for shielding the wearer's complexion and eyes from the glaring western sun, the pioneer sunbonnet was worn by American farm and ranch women and those who crossed the Great Plains in the 19th century. Worn assiduously by our great-grandmothers and grandmothers, the sunbonnet was a distinctly American garment. Women have always worn bonnets of some sort, but the pioneer sunbonnet was exceptional because it had such a deep brim.

Several years ago, I created The Pioneer Sunbonnet exhibit, which highlighted nineteen Texas sunbonnets from the 19th and early 20th century. From the late 19th century black batiste mourning bonnet to the simple 1930s flour sack cotton models, the viewer quickly perceives the down-to-earth spirit of our pioneer ancestors.

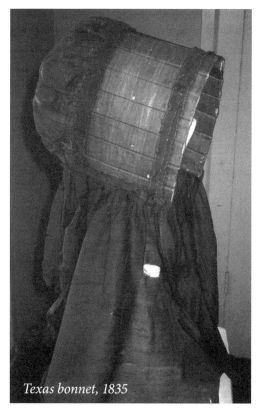

Texas bonnet, 1835

Because sunbonnets are usually homemade, they are difficult to date with any exactitude. One of the most interesting numbers is a Texas sunbonnet from the Heritage Collection of HWF. I once showed it to the noted fashion curator of the Houston Museum of Fine Arts, Elizabeth Ann Coleman, who authoritatively dated it as far back as 1835.

Generally speaking, the sunbonnet boasted a deep brim often with a ruffle around the front and sides. A capelike portion, called a 'bavolet' or curtain at the back, protected the nape of the wearer's neck. The bavolet might vary in length from 3" to 15". Ties under the chin would hold the entire piece in place.

When creating her own sunbonnet, a woman found that her greatest challenge was to achieve enough stiffness in the brim so that it wouldn't collapse. This could

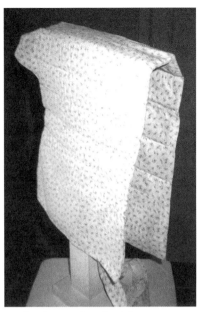

Author's grandmother's bonnet, 1935

be achieved in several ways. Sometimes, multiple layers of fabric, including one of crinoline or buckram, were stitched by hand or treadle sewing machine (on the market by mid-19th century) in dozens of tiny quilted lines and designs. Some were stitched in squares, diamonds, curves, or hexagonal design. The creator was limited only by her own imagination and availability of materials.

Goods used were as diverse as the women who made them: calico, coarse muslin, checked gingham, pique, feed sack cotton, chambray, sateen, fine sheer wool crepe, and silk taffeta. Trims varied from eyelet lace to rickrack, the first commercial braid to be on the market. Occasionally, the brim of a sunbonnet was given a lining of a different color. For practical purposes, many bonnets were quickly sewn and left unembellished. Sometimes a woman might have the leisure to embroider designs on the brim or to crochet lace edging. The important role of mourning during Victorian times was indicated by the presence of a black sunbonnet in most women's wardrobes.

Another stiffening technique was to sew multiple casings in the brim. Lightweight strips of hickory wood were slipped into the casings and this was called a slat sunbonnet. Later, women cut cardboard strips to insert in these casings. When it was necessary to wash a soiled bonnet, the wearer removed the wood or cardboard before laundering. Then, after starching and ironing the bonnet, the slats of hickory or strips of cardboard could be re-inserted. If the wearer deemed the old cardboard strips too limp, she could just cut new ones from a cardboard box. A pioneer sunbonnet was the very essence of practicality.

By the 1890s, sunbonnets could be ordered by mail. Montgomery Ward & Co. sold a checked percale number with lace edging for twenty-five cents. Since little girls always wore miniature models of the

Heritage Collection, 1930s

sunbonnet, the catalog featured a child's model that could be had for fifteen cents.

Exterior photographs from the frontier almost always show women and girls

Feed sack cotton
1930s

wearing sunbonnets or some sort of wide-brimmed hat, even when riding a horse. Betty J. Mills in her *Calico Chronicle*, Texas Tech Press, quotes a Mrs. Sinks who wrote in 1840 of an unfortunate experience: "Instead of acting with the usual good sense of frontier people, wearing sunbonnets, we donned little riding caps. We were not exactly roasted when we came back, but we brought with us a resplendent set of faces."

WHEN BUSTER BROWN CAME TO TOWN

Were you there when Buster Brown came to town? A popular line of children's shoes from the Brown Shoe Company, Buster Brown is probably America's best-known brand of children's shoes.

My mother, born in the early days of the 20th century, always told the story of Buster Brown's coming to town. It was Dallas, Texas and a young midget played the part of Buster Brown, with a Dutch boy haircut and wearing a tam-o-shanter. Mother could remember as a child, being utterly fascinated with this "little boy" who could dance and sing so well. She was so young that she truly believed that he was Buster Brown.

A Waco woman told a similar story. Thelma Day Hall grew up in the little country town of Hico, Texas at the turn of the century. Her uncle owned the mercantile store on the town square. One bustling Saturday afternoon, when all the farmers and their families were in town, Buster Brown suddenly appeared on the flat roof of the mercantile store. He called out to everyone and then began to sing and dance there on the rooftop. Afterward, inside the store, Thelma's father bought her a pair of little red Buster Brown high-buttoned boots that had a tassel at each ankle.

I, myself, wore Buster Brown shoes throughout childhood. Sometimes, it was a pair of sturdy oxfords; another time it might be a pair of patent leather Mary Janes. I vividly remember the pleasure of being allowed to wear brand new shoes home from the store, while staring down at them all the way. Mom always bought our shoes at Goldstein-Migel's on Austin Avenue, and I can remember how my sister and I loved to play with the X-ray machine there. When I had my daughter in the 1960s, I began buying Buster Brown shoes for her.

My sister Emily, who also wore Buster Brown shoes, sported a Buster Brown haircut. During the 1930s, this was a very popular style. Emily was a feisty little tomboy and the straight bangs and short bob suited the kid just perfectly.

118

Brown Shoe Company was founded by George Warren Brown in 1878 in St. Louis, Missouri. He chose the site wisely since that area ultimately became a manufacturing center for America's shoe industry. The company is now a major international corporation, producing several popular shoe lines, including the enduring Buster Brown line.

The original Buster Brown was a mischievous cartoon character who delighted children of all ages. His creator was Richard F. Outcault. The Buster Brown shoe brand began when St. Louis was the site of the 1904 World's Fair. An enterprising young Brown Shoe executive met Buster Brown's creator there and purchased the licensing rights for $200.

Brown Shoe Company made marketing history when it began to send out road shows with actors who were really midgets dressed as Buster Brown. Each actor was accompanied by a dog since the comic strip character always was shown with a dog named Tige. Touring the entire country to promote Buster Brown shoes, these diminutive actors performed in theaters, department stores, and shoe stores. In the early days of the 20th century, such a free show generally attracted the entire town.

In 1917, Brown Shoe Company launched a national advertising campaign for Buster Brown shoes. It was the first line of children's shoes to be marketed in popular magazines such as *The Saturday Evening Post* and *Ladies' Home Journal*. This successful campaign established Buster Brown as a national brand.

In the 1940s, Buster Brown brand was promoted on a children's radio show called The Buster Brown Gang. Later, the Buster Brown Gang moved on to Saturday morning television shows with Smilin' Ed, Andy Devine, and Captain Kangaroo. In the latter part of the 20th century, Buster Brown was associated with Walt Disney movies and was even endorsed by Olympic track star Bruce Jenner in 1979. In 1982, the company licensed the movie character E.T. for E.T. Shoes by Buster Brown. In 2004, Buster Brown celebrated its 100th anniversary. Over the decades, shoe styles have changed, but the name of Buster Brown endures.

PERSONALITIES

THE CALLING CARD: A VICTORIAN SOCIAL NECESSITY

Like so many other points of etiquette, the calling card was a custom born in France and exported to this continent. As far back as the 18th century, people of note carried the calling card, a narrow sliver of engraved cardstock. While visiting the Musée Château Ramezay in Montreal, Canada, I saw an elegant silk and velour cardholder once owned by the Baroness Josepha de Germain. It was dated 1755.

Collectibles today, these little calling card cases might have been crafted of silver, gold, tortoise shell, mother-of-pearl, wood, or lacquer. As with the baroness from Montreal, it might have been hand-crafted.

During the 19th century, the calling card was one of society's most important means of social communication. Bearing the name and sometimes the address, it was a necessary accoutrement of every socially adept person. Calling cards were used to pay calls, when sending a gift, to send flowers, to post regrets for a reception, or to announce a change of address.

Tucked away in an HWF storage box is a small card that was once used by Miss Mary Kinnard who once lived in Earle-Napier-Kinnard House. It's a good example of the written message on the calling card. This card was found pinned to a lace doily that is also in our collection. Hand-written in pencil, Mary's message says, "This was made by Mrs. P.L. Downs as a wedding gift for Miss Annie Kinnard." Sister Annie was married December 4, 1904.

Among the effects of Claude Barron's great uncle, Dr. I.L. McGlasson are stacks of calling cards that accompanied the many floral tributes sent to the doctor's Waco funeral in 1926: Mr. & Mrs. E. A. Sturgis, Mr. Edward Rice Bolton, Mrs. Edward C. Long, J.R. Torrence, and Mrs. William Cameron. Mrs. Cameron's calling card includes the word, "Thursdays," which meant that she always received visitors on Thursdays.

Call-and-card etiquette ordained the use of calling cards with a slight difference in size and information given. Even among women, size could differ. A married woman used calling cards slightly larger than those of an unwed lady. The names of her unwed daughters might have been listed on her card just beneath her own name. Gentlemen used narrower cards of lighter weight stock to avoid any extra bulge in the shallow front pocket of their fitted waistcoats. An unmarried gentleman still living at his parents' home might add the name of his club where he could also be reached.

According to Ward McAllister, 19th century social arbiter and author of *Society as I Have Found It*, 1890, titles were to be avoided. A lady was either a Miss or a Mrs. He advised that a woman could not properly share on her card the dignities conferred on her husband. The United States' First Lady was simply Mrs. William McKinley. Even if a woman had earned the title of Dr., she could not affix the title to her personal card. She was advised by Mr. McAllister to use a separate business card giving her name, title, address, and office hours.

In the 19th century, many a woman held open house on a specific day, finding it convenient to have this information printed on her personal calling card. As with Mrs. William Cameron, a mere "Thursdays" would indicate that she would be receiving every Thursday. If you were in the know, you knew.

Properly used, a calling card was given to the servant at the door or sent to the door via a carriage footman. The visitor would wait while the card was shown to the hostess who would read it and beckon the visitor to come into her drawing room or perhaps she would send word that she was not receiving. In this instance, the visitor would just leave the calling card.

Every household would have a small decorative tray or basket near the front door where these calling cards were gathered. At day's end, the lady of the house could sift through the accumulated cards to see who had been by. The system served the same purpose as our answering machine today.

And then there was the subject of death. Victorian mourning traditions were taken very seriously, and calling cards reflected those attitudes. A third of an inch black border on her calling card was deemed appropriate mourning for a widow. Every six month period, this border could be snipped with scissors a sixteenth of an inch until mourning was put off entirely. We know that the widowed Mrs. William Aldredge Fort of Waco, remained in mourning for the rest of her life. Her black-bordered calling card would have reflected this fact.

One popular calling card practice was the turned-down corner, which hinted at certain messages. A folded down top left corner meant that the caller had arrived in person. If left unfolded, a servant had most likely delivered it to the house. This card-folding craze with all its many local variations fell out of favor by the 1920s. A tray full of mutilated calling cards was an unsightly thing, in any case.

A universal calling card practice for persons who planned a long trip was to leave cards with all friends and relatives to notify them of their absence The letters P.P.C. stood for *pour prendre congé*, which means to take leave. They were hand-written in a lower corner and sometimes the destination city and hotel were also included.

It was Mrs. Herbert Hoover in the 1930s who balked at the leaving of cards in Washington, D.C. As wife of the Secretary of Commerce under President Warren Harding and later as First Lady, Lou Hoover resolved to eliminate that outdated tradition. Previously, there was an absolute blizzard of calling cards four or five afternoons a week, each one requiring a hand-written acknowl-edgment. This level-headed, socially self-assured woman secured a mutual agreement among the other cabinet wives that calling cards would not be used anymore. This, plus the general use of the telephone as a more efficient means of communication, spelled the end of the calling card.

Yet, Emily Post, the 20th century's most famous etiquette authority, devotes 18 pages to calling card usage in her 1950 edition. A 1970 etiquette writer, Amy Vanderbilt, informs us that, while the calling card has almost disappeared, it is still used in conservative circles such as the military and diplomatic corps. She devotes more than a dozen pages to all the possibilities of the calling card. In altered form, this tradition still survives: the business card.

THE POWER OF THE CALLING CARD

The most vivid example of the power of the calling card involved two New York City matrons who locked horns over an invitation to a ball. In 1883, Mrs. William Kissam Vanderbilt—a woman of the most fiery temperament and insatiable social ambition—built the biggest and most lavishly-furnished house in the city. To show it off to New York society, she planned a costume ball that is still considered the most sumptuous affair ever given there.

Mrs. William Kissam Vanderbilt

Unfortunately, the one social lioness she most wanted to impress was Mrs. William Backhouse Astor, Jr. Here was a woman of impeccable Schermerhorn lineage and old wealth. Concerned with the influx of *nouveaux riches* outsiders, Mrs. Astor and her major domo of entertainment, the redoubtable Ward McAllister, had created a guest list of 400 of the *crème de la crème* of society popularly known as "Mrs. Astor's 400." It certainly did not include the parvenus Vanderbilts.

Mrs. Vanderbilt, who was as cunning and determined as Attilla the Hun, threw down a challenge to Mrs. Astor, choosing a Monday evening for her ball. Now, it was a well-known fact that Monday evenings traditionally belonged to Mrs. Astor. Mrs. Vanderbilt had 1500 invitations printed, mailing all but one that she purposely held back.

During the plans for the ball, Mrs. Vanderbilt just happened to discover that her daughter had innocently invited Mrs. Astor's daughter. "My dear, I have never been received by Mrs. Astor. Her child may not be a guest in our house!" Both girls were reduced to tears, but cold-hearted Mrs. Vanderbilt staunchly held her ground.

Besieged by a wailing daughter, Mrs. Astor finally relented. Donning a Charles Frederick Worth afternoon gown, she had herself driven to the Vanderbilt mansion. Remaining in the coach, she handed one of her precious calling cards to her coachman and waited while he marched up to the front door and handed it to Mrs.Vanderbilt's butler who, in turn, handed it to the triumphant Mrs. Vanderbilt. Only a few minutes after Mrs. Astor returned home, a Vanderbilt servant hand-delivered that last invitation to the ball of the century.

Mrs. William Backhouse Astor, Jr.

JACOB DE CORDOVA–DREAMER OF DREAMS

O f all the new settlers to Texas after the 1836 battle of San Jacinto, Jacob de Cordova (born 1808) emerges as one of the most memorable. Eminently qualified to help in the development of this new republic, he was a writer and a talented printer with a background in civil engineering and geology. He spoke English, Hebrew, French, Spanish, and German. This facility with languages would later enable him to learn several Indian dialects.

The de Cordova family claimed descendancy from nobles of the l5th century court of King Ferdinand of Spain. Driven out of Spain because of the Inquisition, they had migrated to Kingston, Jamaica to become English subjects. By 1819, the de Cordovas were living in Philadelphia, Pennsylvania.

In 1826, young Jacob married a member of a pioneer Philadelphia family, Rebecca Sterling. She was of the Baptist faith and most likely, he was Jewish. Five children were born of this marriage: William, Frances, Henry, Jinney, Elizabeth, and Joshua.

Because of health problems, Jacob sought a warmer climate and moved his growing family to New Orleans. Hearing of all the possibilities in the new Republic of Texas, he came here, bringing merchandise to the settlers while looking into the situation. By 1839, he had moved his family to the Texas port of entry, Galveston, where he appeared before a magistrate to become a naturalized citizen.

In 1848, de Cordova was employed to lay out a town adjacent to the Brazos River, taking an undivided one fifth interest in the land as his payment. Together with George Erath, he surveyed and developed Waco Village that ultimately came to be known as Waco, the county seat of McLennan County.

He, Rebecca, and the children soon moved on to the more populous city of Houston that would be the family home for the next fourteen years. With his knowledge of the intricate land laws of Texas as well as an intimate acquaintance with the land systems under the Spanish, Mexican, and American governments, this personable young man began to build one of the largest land agencies Texas would ever know. Always intrigued with the possibilities to the west where he saw good, rich land for the taking, he moved to Seguin, the county seat of Guadalupe County. The year was 1851.

By 1858, having traveled over much of the state, de Cordova was a recognized authority on Texas. He was called upon to deliver lectures to organizations in eastern cities of the United States, including the New York Geographical Society. He was invited by the Cotton Supply Association of Manchester, England to travel there and lecture on cotton growing in Texas. The general theme was Texas as a new home for emigrants.

Always employing his writing skills to help his home state, de Cordova published many guidebooks and pamphlets promoting Texas and the possibilities of cotton cultivation here. He produced several valuable maps of Texas for newcomers and travelers, always revising them when new information was available. He was associated with the publishing of newspapers in Kingston, Jamaica, Houston, and Austin.

As with many land speculators, Jacob de Cordova's fortunes rose and fell as his land holdings were pared away by lawsuits. Ever the public booster though, he was a generous donor of land to churches and schools. Even into his later years after the Civil War, he was planning a project on the Brazos River in Bosque County that would have provided power to cotton mills and other manufacturing enterprises.

All these cherished dreams were cut short by death in 1868. He and Rebecca, who died in 1882, were buried in a cemetery near Kimball's Bend. In 1935, both bodies were removed to the State Cemetery in Austin where many other Texas pioneers now rest. Despite his business acumen, de Cordova did not leave a will. Seventeen years would pass before his tangled affairs were settled by a succession of administrators.

All of the above information was taken from the book, *Jacob de Cordova, Land Merchant of Texas* by James M. Day who wrote his master's thesis on the subject when he was a graduate student at the University of Texas in the late 1950s. The largest source for his thesis was the collection of de Cordova's letters, which now reside in the Texas State Archives.

ROBERT E. LEE

Among the pantheon of our country's military heroes, the name Robert E. Lee (born 1807) looms large. Even though his charismatic leadership failed to save the South, every Confederate sympathizer revered his memory. His framed image was displayed in many a Southern home. All the families of our four Historic Waco Foundation house museums were aligned with the Confederacy. Each house today appropriately features a framed image of the great man.

Initially, Texans had been asked to vote on leaving the Union and joining the Confederacy. The air was hot with war fever as Sam Houston appeared in Waco to campaign against Texas' joining the Confederacy. One can almost picture all those young Texians who were so eager to fight the Yankees. Because Houston's argument was so unwelcomed, bodyguards were required to protect him from the wrath of the crowds as he campaigned throughout Texas.

Back east as war was being declared, Lee sent word to his wife, Mary Anna Randolph Custis Lee, at Arlington to leave the place immediately and not allow herself to be taken captive. As a direct descendant of Martha Custis Washington, Mrs. Lee was the legal owner of Arlington House. Hastily, she piled wagons full of precious Washington-Custis memorabilia and drove off just before Union troops arrived. The troops ransacked Arlington and piled furniture on wagons and had a fine spectacle of a parade through the capitol city. In a spiteful move, federal troops occupied the house and began to bury its war dead right up to the front door. As a result, neither Lee nor his progeny would ever be able to live in the house again. The house and all its acreage is now known as Arlington National Cemetery.

Lee's decision to declare for the southern cause was considered by many to be especially traitorous. He was a West Point graduate and had served as Superintendent there. As a junior officer in the United States Army, he had fought shoulder-to-shoulder in the Mexican-American War of 1846-48 with many of his classmates, some who would later declare for the south, some for the north. Among them were Ulysses S. Grant, George Meade, George B. McClellan, Ambrose Burnside, Stonewall Jackson, James Longstreet, and the future president of the Confederacy, Jefferson Davis.

At war's end, General Lee arrived at the McLean home at Appomadox, VA to sign the surrender document. He was dressed appropriately, with a high polish on his old boots, a carefully brushed uniform, and his jewel-handled dress sword. General Grant, who was casually dressed at the time, said later that when he saw that sword, he began to think of all the Confederate officers and the hardships they were going to suffer in the future. It was he who suggested adding a generous proviso in the surrender that would allow all Confederate officers to keep their swords and their horses.

A treasured memento of Robert E. Lee can be seen at Fort House. It's a small framed autographed photo of Lee. It seems as though he began to autograph such photos for the price of $5 after the war. Retired from his wartime duties, Lee served as president of a men's school, Washington College, in Lexington, VA until his death in 1870. The profits from those photographs went into a building fund for the school, which had suffered along with the rest of the South.

Idolized by Southerners and grudgingly respected by Northerners, Lee went on to rebuild the school. His name, always associated with honesty and integrity, attracted top teachers and many new students. The school thrived under his capable leadership and would ultimately be renamed Washington and Lee University in his memory. His tomb is located in the school chapel.

With a family to care for and funds tight during his years as university president, Lee chose not to outfit himself in expensive new civilian clothes. So he had his wife remove all evidence of military rank from his old gray frock coat. She covered each gilt military button with black fabric. A modest man to the end, gentleman Robert E. Lee had no need of gold braid and epaulettes to declare his fame.

THE SOCIETY OF THE CINCINNATI

One of the most prestigious and exclusive fraternal orders of our country is the Society of the Cincinnati, officers who fought or served in the Revolutionary War. Honoring George Washington, it was organized on May 10, 1783 at Fishkill, New York. Within a year, branches of the Society were established in all thirteen states as well as France. George Washington himself served as the organization's first President General until his death in 1799.

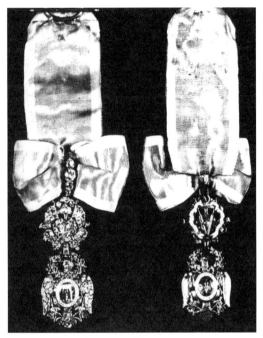

Its original membership numbered 2,150, about half of those eligible to join the organization. Two hundred of them were French. To qualify, an officer must have served to the end of the war, resigned with honor after a minimum of three years of service, or to have been honorably discharged after three years of service. Following the rule of primogeniture, the membership was to pass to the eldest son. Lacking a son, a collateral male descendant, if properly qualified, could take up membership.

The Diamond Eagle of the Cincinnatti, front and back.

Every original member, and every prospective member, can be represented in the Society today by a descendant. It also accepts descendants of officers who were killed in battle or died in service and therefore had no chance to join after the Revolutionary War. Currently, the American and French Societies have nearly 3,500 active members.

Initially, the new Society was not without controversy. Many considered it an elitist organization. Those with democratic hopes for the newly emerging country became anxious about the possibility of a developing nobility. We have to remember that the United States Constitution was not ratified until 1788. There were some citizens who favored patterning the new American government after that of England, with a king (George Washington perhaps) and a parliament, an idea which the great man quickly discouraged.

It is interesting to trace the names of the many adventurous foreigners who crossed the Atlantic to support our revolt against England and King George. Every history buff knows of General von Steuben who barked out orders in a heavy Germanic accent. Today, Americans honor the young Marquis de Lafayette who was denied official passage out of France by Louis XVI. He then secretly purchased a ship, loaded it with all his compatriots, and gayly sailed for America. In acknowledgment of his contributions, both military and financial, to our revolution two hundred years ago, Congress just recently accorded honorary U.S. citizenship to the Marquis de Lafayette.

Admiral de Grasse also sailed from France. His fleet obstructed General Cornwallis at Yorktown in a battle ensuring Washington's victory and ended the war. Comte de Rochambeau was sent by the French king with 6,000 regulars who took part in that final battle at Yorktown. There were Polish nobles such as Colonel Thadeuz Kosciuszko and an exile from the Czar's court, Baron Gustavus Heinrich von Wetter-Rosendahl, who fought under the assumed name Major John Rose.

For these foreigners, it must have been one of the greatest adventures of their lives, being able to participate in the founding of a new nation. Americans should never forget the debt we owe the French and others. General Washington, with his exhausted army, was the first to admit that the war would have been lost if Admiral de Grasse's fleet hadn't been there that fateful day at Yorktown, October 17, 1781. Faithful young Lafayette had fought with Washington throughout the war and was present at the surrender.

Among many gifts to Historic Waco Foundation by the sisters Ida and Emma Morris is a certificate of the Cincinnati. Still retaining its beautiful hand-tinting, it shows the signature of the Society's first President General, George Washington. The individual to whom it was designated was Polish; unfortunately, his name is no longer decipherable. This precious framed document hung on a wall at Fort House

Museum for many years before it was conserved. It now rests in safe climate and humidity-controlled storage.

The Society's insignia, inspired by the American eagle, was created by Major Pierre Charles L'Enfant, whose designs were later used to lay out the city of Washington. The Diamond Eagle of the Society of the Cincinnati was first worn by George Washington. Each succeeding President General is entitled to wear it while in office.

The Society's name comes from antiquity. In the fifth century BC, there was a great Roman military leader named Lucius Quinctius Cincinnatus. As with George Washington, he led his armies against Rome's enemies time after time. And similar to Washington, he longed to retire on his farm to enjoy the rustic life. The Society's motto says it all for both heroes: "Omnia relinquit servare rempublicam" which means "He gave up everything to serve the republic."

THE TRIP OF A LIFETIME

During the centennial year of 1876, the entire Fort family, two adults and their seven adolescent children, took the trip of a lifetime. Surviving family letters tell us that Mr. and Mrs. William A. Fort made their way from Waco to Virginia where all the children were in school—the five boys at Virginia Military Institute and the two girls at Wesleyan Female Institute.

From there, they all traveled to Washington, D.C. One can only imagine the thrill of being able to view the great city and all its historical buildings. The family may have visited the newly opened Museum of Natural History, already renowned for its exhibitions and scientific holdings. No doubt the Smithsonian Institution, begun in 1846, would have been on the Fort "wish" list to visit. Nearby was Lincoln Park, recently opened to the public.

But, looking back from today's perspective, one would wonder about the adults' feelings as they strolled along the great walkways of the Washington, D.C. mall. After all, William Fort had fought for the Confederacy a little more than a decade before. The younger generation would have missed the war years, but for Mr. Fort to see the Yankee capital thriving when the south was still reeling from wartime devastation must have been a shock.

Venturing farther into Yankee land, the family stopped in Philadelphia, which was celebrating the centennial of the United States with a great fair. Twenty-six states and eleven nations took part in one of the most successful world's fairs ever. Spanning the months between May and November of that celebratory year, the fair was attended by more than ten million visitors, many from foreign lands.

There, the Forts saw the right arm and torch of the future Statue of Liberty on display. For fifty cents, a visitor could climb its interior ladder to a balcony that over-looked all the fair-grounds. The profits from this exhibit went toward the finishing of the statue. It

wouldn't be assembled and dedicated for another ten years, but at least Americans could see the beginning of the famous statue that never fails to impress visitors to New York City harbor today.

New scientific advances were on display at the fair, such as Alexander Graham Bell's telephone, the Remington typewriter, Heinz ketchup, Hires root beer, the Corliss steam engine, and the English bicycle. You can just imagine how much the Fort young folks enjoyed seeing firsthand the new inventions that would ultimately influence their own futures. Prophetically, the Turkish delegation introduced a new substance to America: marijuana, which attracted some of the biggest crowds of the fair.

Creators of the fair had hoped that it would help heal the wounds left from the Civil War. One stipulation of the fair was that no political or offensive reference could be made to that conflict. Few southern states had chosen to join the centennial celebration, most likely because they were still suffering from the financial strains of the war.

Traveling farther north, the Fort family arrived in New York City. "The Greatest Show on Earth," produced by P.T. Barnum, dominated the entertainment scene. The Metropolitan Museum of Art was just beginning to develop and wouldn't be open to the public until 1880, but nearby was the beginning of Central Park designed by Frederick Olmsted. For folks from small town Waco, Texas, the sounds and sights of the great, bustling metropolis must have been a heady experience indeed.

As an added treat, the Forts took the two girls to Tiffany's, where each was invited to choose a piece of jewelry. Nineteen-year-old Mary chose a gold necklace, which can be seen in her photo-portrait hanging in Fort House today. From a surviving family letter, we know the white batiste gown that she wore for that photo-sitting was purchased in New York on the same trip.

After several weeks on the road, the family returned to Waco. The photo-portraits of Mary and Mr. Fort were made and hand-tinted. Both now hang in Fort House Museum. Mrs. Fort may have sat for her portrait, but we don't know of the photograph's whereabouts.

Unfortunately, the aftermath of that dream trip proved to be most devastating. Insidiously and without warning, typhoid fever visited Fort House and suddenly, young Mary Fort was dead. She had been the apple of her father's eye, an accomplished young woman of great promise. Months later, Fort himself succumbed, most likely of a heart attack. The other children matured and left the nest. Mrs. Fort, who dressed in widow's weeds for the rest of her life, died in 1910. The entire family is buried in the Fort family plot in Oakwood Cemetery.

THE NUCLEUS OF THE
SMITHSONIAN INSTITUTION COLLECTION

With acute foresight, the Smithsonian Institution sent a special representative to the Philadelphia centennial celebration. Young Spencer Fullerton Baird, a naturalist on the staff, was sent to oversee the Smithsonian exhibit and all the other U.S. government exhibits as well. All along, he was wisely ingratiating himself with the directors of all the other exhibits. As the fair came to an end, most of the exhibits, even foreign ones, were open-handedly given to Baird for the Smithsonian.

It's reported that Baird sent off sixty freight cars to Washington, D.C. filled with this bonanza. Many exhibits would find their way into the Arts & Industries Building and the National Museum of Natural History. Spencer Fullerton Baird served as curator and the second secretary of the Smithsonian Institution. He devoted his career to creating one of the world's great collections. This information was provided by Dr. Pamela Henson, Specialist at the Smithsonian Institution.

UNDER THE CHRISTMAS TREE

When I was a little girl, I always knew that every year there would be a doll for me under the Christmas tree. Somehow, the holiday celebration became identified with a new doll, a beautiful lady doll, or perhaps a cuddly baby doll. This must have been true for many little girls.

It was all part of that childhood enchantment of tinsel and lights, Baby Jesus in a *crèche* on the mantel, caroling, and eating a big Christmas dinner with my cousins in Grandmother's kitchen. All the adults sat around the formal oval table in the dining room, but we kids knew the warm, cozy kitchen was the best place to sneak extra servings of pie or cake.

My baby sister, Emily, and I had been led to believe in Santa Claus and every year, we would lie in bed, listening intently for the sound of sleigh bells as Santa visited Christmas Eve. We were sure that we would be able to catch him in the act, but somehow, we always fell asleep before the old fellow arrived with his gifts.

Nevertheless, Santa always came through with a thoughtfully-chosen doll along with other gifts. One especially memorable Christmas morning, my extra gift was a small blue leatherette case that opened to reveal a hand-wound record player inside. It had only one record, *Somewhere Over the Rainbow* sung by Judy Garland—every kid's heroine from Wizard of Oz. I played it so many times that I learned all the words and could warble along with Judy.

That year my doll was Shirley Temple with blond curls, rosy cheeks, and those trademark dimples. Of course, Shirley was one of my favorite movie stars and my mother always arranged my thick curls with a big ribbon bow just like Shirley's. Mother, who must have enjoyed such challenges, created an elegant satin-lined fur coat for Shirley from an old muff and closed the collar with a glittery rhinestone clasp. I must have been the only girl in Dallas to have a custom-made fur coat for her Shirley Temple. This lovely doll met her fate one night when she fell out of my bed and cracked her skull open. I mourned that loss for days.

Another Christmas doll was Princess Elizabeth with a smile that always seemed a wee bit distant. After all, she was a real princess. Everyone knew all about the two little daughters of the King of England who were just a bit older than Emily and I. I always wondered if the two royal sisters argued and rough housed the same as we did.

I guess my favorite was Betsy Wetsy, an innovative doll made of rubber with a tiny hole in her lips and another at her bottom. She came with a little suitcase of clothes, extra diapers, and a rubber-tipped nursing bottle. I remember that Christmas day when my sister and I hung our dolls' wet diapers over the fireplace screen to dry in front of the fire. To my delight, Betsy could be given a bath like a real baby. Mother used to add a few drops of bluing to the water, making a colorful bath for us and our dolls as we played in the bubbles.

Many of those Christmas dolls came from the old Goldstein-Migel's on Austin Avenue. Visiting Goldstein's holiday displays was a ritual, a breath-taking experience for a starry-eyed child. Among all the other toys such as trains, trucks, erector sets, and Lincoln logs, there were always dozens of pretty dolls to choose from.

Today, a large assortment of antique dolls from the past can be viewed at Historic Waco Foundation's Earle-Napier-Kinnard House Museum. We have almost forty dolls of various sizes, manufacturers, and types on display there. Some of our more delicate dolls are kept in the storage area of Hoffmann House along with our Heritage Collection.

Always anxious to refine the documentation of our collection, several years ago I set up a project wherein each doll would be carefully analyzed, evaluated, and photographed. In order to do a good job, I knew I had to find an expert on the subject. I am well versed in the history of clothing and can distinguish one period from another, but I know very little about dolls.

Historic Waco Foundation was fortunate to have the volunteer help of a local doll collector, expert, and dealer, Pauline Winston. We are very grateful to have had her expertise on this project. She was able to point out many details that we had missed in our original accessioning.

Our collection is an assortment of dolls made in many countries: Germany, Japan, France, Hong Kong, and America. All sorts of materials such as sawdust, straw, composition, canvas, wood, or hard rubber were used to make a body. Heads, feet, and hands were made from bisque, paper-maché, china, composition, or leather. There are baby dolls, lady dolls, rag dolls, and even a boy doll. Our smallest doll is just six inches and one of the largest is three feet, just about the size of a small child. Dates range from 1870 to 1950.

Studying these old dolls evokes childhood memories of playing house, cuddling, scolding, and spanking my precious dollies. They were my favorite form of play. Even when our family visited our Waco grandmother in the summertime and my dolls had been left at home, my clever mother would make corncob dolls for us.

From scraps of cotton fabric and lace, she would fashion tiny dresses and bonnets for the corncob, then draw on eyes and lips for the face. These were rustic substitutes for the refined Shirley Temple or Betsy Wetsy dolls, nothing you'd ever find under a Christmas tree, but were actually more of a challenge to a child's imagination.

WHEN TRAVEL WAS POSH

One of the most elegant objects in the Heritage Collection of HWF is a small valise, circa 1930s. An overnight bag, it measures 6"deep x 15" x 21". It's made of black leather with solid brass clasps and a dark green textured leather lining. As was the custom of the times, it has its own specially tailored gray canvas removable cover to protect its fine leather exterior.

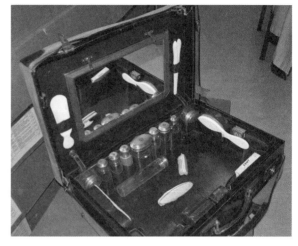

Emblazoned on the canvas cover are the initials of the owner, PFS, Pauline Foster Stephens, 1892-1970. Evidently, it was given to her by her brother, John H. Foster of San Antonio, Texas. Sometime after her death, he donated it to Historic Waco Foundation.

In the early days of the 20th century, a stylish woman always traveled with carefully selected matched luggage. For train travel, Pauline would have been dressed up in full regalia with hat, gloves, high heels, silk stockings, furs, and what have you. This overnight bag might have been part of a complete set of matched luggage, including a steamer trunk for ocean cruises.

You can almost imagine Pauline, enjoying a glamorous adventure on the Orient Express between the world wars. This valise would have been perfectly appropriate on that terribly posh train. Her fellow travelers might have been spies and blackguards, but they were always perfectly dressed and outfitted with elegant luggage.

Open up this little travel gem and you find more than twenty-five personal toiletry articles arranged all along the inside periphery. The empty center is meant to hold overnight garments such as nightgown, robe, and slippers.

Glancing through the August 1931 *Harper's Bazaar* magazine, I discovered a valise similar to Pauline's. It held the cosmetic preparations of Elizabeth Arden, one of the pioneers of the cosmetic industry. It must have been a most deluxe edition since the jeweler, Cartier, had fitted all the jars and bottles with sterling silver tops.

Each article in Pauline's valise has its own fitted space or strap to hold it in place. On the underside of the suitcase lid is a large removable brass-edged mirror. There is a shoe horn and a form for shaping laundered gloves. There are a set of three hair combs and several brushes: a shoe brush, clothes brush, hairbrush, and nailbrush, all with Bakelite backs. A long narrow crystal tube with gilt top would have held the requisite toothbrush.

For manicure purposes, there is a nail polisher with its own detachable mole-skin cover. There are a dozen or so gilt-topped crystal jars of various sizes and shapes meant to hold perfume, creams, face powder, etc.

Pauline was a smoker, evidently. We found an empty Kent cigarette packet and matches tucked into a corner, along with a very posh carved ivory cigarette holder. To while away the time in her train compartment, she could have resorted to a dual set of playing cards in a green leather holder.

There is a flat green leather wallet for money and a small velvet-lined jewelry box to hold her rings and earrings overnight. The most intriguing accoutrement is the foldable curling iron and its own Bunsen burner, each enclosed in its own green leather case.

In small gilt letters on the underside of the suitcase is the name E. Hofmann, supposedly the manufacturer. The smallest item in Pauline's suitcase is a tiny matching snapped purse that holds the little key to the case. Considering the contents, the entire case is understandably heavy, but not to worry. The Red Cap would be happy to help!

YOUTH AT WORK AND AT PLAY

It's been a century since Fort House has seen little children running and laughing in its backyard; and ages since childish chatter rang through the old place. Somehow, I think Fort House was pleased to have children there again one week during the summer of 2010.

YESTERDAY AND TODAY SUMMER CAMP proved to be a very successful introduction for young children to learn about Victorian life. This event was the brainchild of Linda Baker. "I wanted to show the children how difficult the simplest tasks were when there was no electricity. Cooking and cleaning were so physically demanding. Self-sufficiency was mandatory. Most food had to be grown on the land since there were few grocery stores. People got up with the sun and went to bed when it set."

When William and Dionitia lived in the handsome brick building at Fourth and Webster in the late 19th century, there were seven children. Four were their own and three were the children of Mr. Fort's sister, Martha Sandal Fort, and William Pickney Downs. The Forts and the Downs had traveled from La Grange, Alabama to Waco in the same wagon train. Tragically, the Downs couple died when their three children were small and the Forts took them in and reared them as their own. Overnight, the Fort family almost doubled in number.

It wasn't unusual that the Forts ended up with a large family full of cousins. Many people today can look back into their family histories and see orphaned family members who were brought up by a loving grandmother. No one would have wanted a family member to be banished to an orphanage.

So just this last July, Fort House hosted thirteen children, average age of eight, who spent every morning of one week experiencing various aspects of life as it might have been lived by the Fort children. We had two boys and eleven girls. It's been a long time since I worked with children, but I must say that those boys and girls, so full of energy and mischief, interacted easily with nary a touch of dissension.

One of the biggest treats for our young guests was the recently-redecorated Penelope Playhouse. This charming little building, not original to the house, but moved there from another Waco location, sits in the backyard of Fort. (The little hand-painted sign on the house front refers to Penelope, Texas where Bobbie Barnes was born.) None of the furnishings are of any historic value, so we just unlocked the door and allowed the kids to run in and out. They developed a secret password and played with all the dolls, little doll furniture, and shabby old toys, many of them from our Attic Treasures sales.

At one point, Linda admonished them to pull out all the furnishings and we would clean house. Oh, they loved the idea. They pulled everything out onto the lawn so that the walls and brick floor could be swept clean of all the accumulated dust and spider webs.

On the little plate rails were all sorts of stray saucers and tiny butter pat plates, some even chipped. I devised an outside table with a board on sawhorses to hold a wash basin of soapy water. Then I gave one of the girls the job of washing all the dishes. She and another child carefully washed and dried and re-set the little plates back on the plate rails. The others were given free reign to replace the furniture as they pleased. So now we have a sparkling clean playhouse, thanks to the children.

Penelope Playhouse

Washing seemed to delight them, so we invited the kids to do a family wash, consisting of socks and dish towels. We filled a big witch's pot with water and the children, up to their arm pits in soap suds, used a scrub board to rub out all the dirt. Then, after rinsing in blue water

(using a couple of drops of Mrs. Stewart's blueing,) they hung everything on a clothesline that had been strung up for that purpose. What fun! What nonsense!

Interior of the Penelope Playhouse

Remembering my own child, I have always known that kids are amazingly inventive when it comes to playtime. Give them a back staircase, a few empty cardboard boxes, leave them alone, and they will create their own fantasy world. Toss a blanket over a table and you've created a cave where they can hide from Indians on the warpath.

Linda Baker, who had a career in teaching, had arranged for several speakers to come and share their expertise with us. Bob Frahm, with years in scouting, showed the kids how to tie various types of knots, a handy skill. Someone demonstrated the technique of sharpening a knife blade on a whetstone. Ellis Bennett, also a former teacher who is steeped in the making of textiles, talked about carding, spinning, and weaving. She showed the children how to card a boll of cotton after the seeds had been pulled out.

HWF president Carl Ballew brought glass canning jars and a load of green beans so the kids could learn how to pickle. One morning, they shelled black-eyed peas, something most had never done before. We shared with each child a length of snake vertebrae, and most of them tied the delicate bones around their wrists with string.

Linda described many of the local birds that can be seen in Texas: the cardinal, the grackle, the robin, the screech owl, humming bird, and the road runner. She emphasized the importance of creating backyard sanctuaries for our Texas songbirds. The kids were invited to tell stories about their own experiences with nature. Each one stood up, walked to the front of the room, and with touching dignity, related some personal experience. All throughout, new words were emphasized and explained so they could be introduced into each child's vocabulary.

Childhood diseases of the past, which have been wiped out by immunization, were described. Polio, mumps, measles, whooping cough, and diphtheria, with all their life-threatening permutations, no longer cripple children and terrorize parents. (We reminded them that young Mary Fort had died at age nineteen from typhoid fever, a disease that is almost unknown in our country today.) Many amusing home remedies and old-fashioned medical practices were discussed. Amazingly, two such remedies such as leeches and cupping are being resurrected by holistic practitioners today.

Another great adventure for the girls was in the "beautification" department: hair rolled on rags. They especially liked the idea of playing hairdresser and rolling each other's hair. The process is simple: the rags are tied on and rolled up when the hair is wet. After the hair dries and the rags are removed, the effect is curly and crinkly.

Then there was the story of the willow toothbrush. I told the children how my Speegleville grandmother always strolled down to the lake every morning to cut a short length of green willow branch, which became her daily toothbrush. That farm lady, who lived to great age, always had perfect teeth. All day, she would chew on the twig until it created a little fuzzy brush on the end.

I have read that the Comanche Indians made a medicinal tea from willow bark, so it makes sense that a willow twig would make a good natural toothbrush. Carl Ballew brought in several willow branches and we cut off little twigs for the kids. The taste was a bit bitter, but it seemed to work. I pointed out that the twig was biodegradable, sanitary, and could be tossed away after one use, as opposed to a toothbrush that is used over and over again.

We offered sack races, using old tow sacks; this was a popular idea. A Lorena youth, Hayden Hendrix, visited one morning and demonstrated his expertise with a unicycle. After all sorts of fancy footwork, he then offered the unicycle to the kids. At first they were a bit timid, but finally they all wanted to give the strange vehicle a try.

The weather was quite warm, of course, so it was suggested that everyone wear a swimsuit one day. When it began to warm up around noontime, the kids ran out and we turned on the lawn sprinklers. I never heard so much laughter. I never saw such a demonstration of pure joy. Sometimes, the simplest things are the grandest. Thirteen little water sprites chasing each other through rainbows of spray, what a sight!

TEXTILES
THE APRON: AN AMERICAN ICON

A few years ago, Historic Waco Foundation announced a new textile exhibit, which was seen at Fort House Museum, Fourth and Webster. Strung from clotheslines and embellishing several manikins were more than fifty of those ubiquitous garments known as aprons, ranging in time from late 19th century to mid-20th century. The exhibit was created by local collector Ellis Bennett.

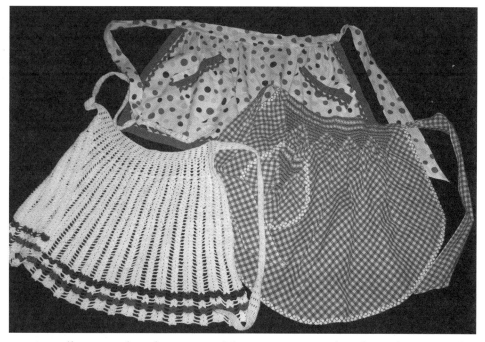

Actually, aprons have been around forever. House workers have alwsays needed some sort of protection from spills and other minor kitchen disasters. Cloth aprons for daily use were made from inexpensive, easy-to-launder fabric or even parts of worn-out clothing. Occupational aprons for nurses, nursemaids, housemaids, or workers in the food industry were also required.

Basic, unembellished styles such as the waist apron, bib apron, and smock apron were desirable; however, women have always loved to put their sewing skills to the test when it came to aprons. Creativity could run the gamut as the seamstress embellished her apron with embroidery, ruffles, quilting, appliqué, lace, and commercial braids such as rickrack.

The waist apron is the most common. It can be long or short, pleated, gored, or flat, gathered tightly or loosely. While there were many commercial patterns to choose from, a clever seamstress could make a simple one without a pattern and individualize it as she pleased. The bib apron has an additional piece of fabric across the chest to give complete protection. It's secured around the neck and tied at the waist. Some aprons of the distant past had bibs that were meant to be pinned to the wearer's dress. The smock apron gives the ultimate protection. It covers the wearer from shoulders to mid-thigh, secured in back with buttons or a simple tie at the back of the neck.

Men's occupational aprons were made from tougher stuff, such as canvas or leather. Blacksmiths, mechanics, and other industrial workers wore aprons suited to the particular task. Restaurant waiters in the past wore ankle-length, white aprons tied around their waists. Today, many occupational workers wear scrubs, overalls, or coveralls instead of aprons.

Aprons are non-discriminatory. Men, women and children wear them, and even babies, if you consider the bib as sort of an apron. Many national costumes include aprons as part of the attire. Even the Masonic Order has an apron included in its regalia. In the very early days of our country, leaders such as George Washington, Benjamin Franklin, and Alexander Hamilton wore such Masonic Order fraternal aprons, usually made of leather.

Sometimes in the past, an apron became a sort of protection from harm. Many family stories of the South tell of folks who posted a Masonic apron on the front door of a home during the Civil War. The power of Masonry was exhibited when a fellow-Mason Union officer showed mercy to the family and saved the house from the torch.

Although the main point of an apron was to protect the more valuable clothing underneath from wear or soil,

George Washington wearing his leather Masonic apron. Lee Lockwood Library and Museum.

women always made sure to have a special Sunday apron to wear when company came to call. Then, the 1950s saw the rise of the party apron. These were colorful confections of voile, organdy, lace, ruffles, ribbons, and embroidery. Sometimes, they were made to match or complement a certain dress the hostess planned to wear at her party. Holiday aprons also became popular. Aprons especially made for Christmas, Valentine's Day, or other such events can often be found by the collector since they were so popular at mid-century.

In the far past, some fashion silhouettes included a purely decorative apron made of silk or fine batiste. The wearer most likely would never have seen the inside of her own kitchen, as in the story of the lady of a great château during the late 18th century French Revolution. Invading the place, the hungry revolutionaries demanded to know the direction of the household kitchen. She innocently replied that she really didn't know where her kitchen was.

The housewife's apron became a symbol. A popular saying, "Tied to his mother's apron strings," was a derogatory comment indicating a man who was helplessly dependent upon his mother. In the 1960s when women began to seriously challenge male authority, young women in the workforce began to disdain the apron as a symbol of oppression and household drudgery.

Nevertheless, the apron still lives on. Men wear them, embellished with silly sayings, as they flip steaks and hamburgers at the backyard barbeque pit. Perhaps now that both men and women are wearing the apron, it will take on new connotations.

Today, aprons are very collectible. Collectors feel that they evoke the very essence of womanhood, of the caring mother and homemaker, even though faded and torn. We can remember our grandmothers and mothers wiping away our tears; the hot pans lifted from the range using layers of apron fabric as a makeshift hot pad; eggs and garden vegetables and sometimes even baby chicks gathered by using the apron skirt as a carryall. I remember my Speegleville grandmother. Every morning, she would tie on the requisite apron as she started breakfast. Along with her ever-present sunbonnet, the apron was part of her regular farm woman regalia.

THE HANDKERCHIEF

Handkerchiefs were used as early as the 2nd century BC in Rome. They used them in the usual manner, but also as a signal when a magistrate would drop a handkerchief to begin the Roman games. They were waved by spectators as a sign of approval. Since then, their function and appearance have altered in response to changes in fashions, social etiquette, and attitudes towards hygiene.

In the early days of the Christian Church, a handkerchief was carried in the left hand of an officiating priest. Finally losing its original identity, it evolved into a simple folded band that by the 12th century, became the *maniple* worn on the left arm.

In the Middle Ages, a knight wore his lady's handkerchief as a symbol of her favor. During the Renaissance, the handkerchief came into general use and was called a *napkyn*.

Initially a large, plain square of fine grade linen, the handkerchief was subsequently embellished with lace or embroidery. It could also be made of silk, cambric, or lawn. It remained a luxury item well into the 17th century.

Oftentimes, a handkerchief can be seen prominently displayed in grand portraiture. In his portrait of the Spanish princess, The Infanta Maria Teresa, the 17th century court painter Velazquez gives her a large square of very sheer linen. It is held by the young princess, draped over one side of her extremely wide skirt. It is a decorative accessory rather than the practical handkerchief, as we know it today.

Then, snuff-taking in the 18th century created a growing need for a more practical handkerchief. The square of lace-edged linen grew smaller, the better to fit inside a gentleman's cuff, handy for covering a discreet sneeze after a whiff of powdered snuff. In order to hide tobacco stains, snuff handkerchiefs were usually dyed brown. It was at this point that brightly colored pictorial or commemorative handkerchiefs were introduced.

Printed handkerchiefs developed in Europe and England simultaneously. All sorts of topics were applied to squares of silk, cotton, and linen: wars, travel, politics, scandal, maps, satire, notable events, royal occasions, celebrities, and nursery rhymes. The Museum of London has among its vast collection of such topical handkerchiefs, colorful examples that celebrate the golden jubilees of King George III (1809) and Queen Victoria (1887).

Up until the late 19th century when hand-weaving was no longer common, linen was a very expensive textile. A fine linen handkerchief would have been a cherished fashion accessory. In his popular novel, *Oliver Twist*, Charles Dickens wrote about the juvenile pickpockets of 19th century London who stole valuable handkerchiefs from gentlemen's tailcoats. Another indication of the handkerchief's value is the fact that Victorians commonly ran newspaper notices requesting the return of lost or stolen handkerchiefs.

The Heritage Collection of HWF has about sixty handkerchiefs, of various sizes and materials. One of our most unusual is a simple white linen square dated about 1940. It is embellished with several rows of initials embroidered in various colors. I believe this oddity served as a salesman's sample. The customer was able to choose the kind of script, including Gothic, Art Deco, and Oriental. All colors seemed to be available, from ecru to deep blue, green, and red. An example of very refined machine monogramming, this handkerchief must be one of several in a series. The sample monograms on this particular handkerchief are numbered from 30 to 41. What happened to the other sample handkerchiefs in this set? It came to HWF as a gift from the Fentress family.

A beautiful example of pre-woven squares of handkerchief-grade linen is a man's handkerchief, dated about 1930. The blue-on-white weave creates an intricate,

tailored design. It is from the Wollett estate and came to the collection in 1988.

The old man with a scythe always hovered nearby in Victorian times and mourning etiquette dictated proper apparel. I have my maternal grand-mother's mourning hand-kerchief—a simple white square of batiste with a black border. One of the most charming handkerchiefs in the HWF collection is a small mourning handkerchief of fine white batiste edged with a wide ruffle of black lace. The woman who carried this lovely hanky must have been wealthy with a strong fashion sense and an appreciation of beautiful things.

Probably the most valuable handkerchief in the Heritage Collection is a simple, little square of ecru silk. All around its four edges runs a single red thread. This is a rare example of a tedious handworking technique called drawnwork in which a single thread of the fabric was tied to a red thread and then pulled clear through. It gives the effect of a red thread having been woven into the material. Wonderful!

Fort House member Dan Capps has his grandmother's handkerchief, which was made in the 1890s. As a little girl, encouraged to practice her needle skills, little Iva Capps was given a scrap of an old salt bag and told to make herself a handkerchief. Iva crocheted a rather handsome lace edging on the fabric, which still has traces of the original Morton Salt printing.

Another handkerchief in our collection was made to celebrate an important occasion in U.S. history, the end of WWI. Just a mere 10" square of pale blue chiffon with a bit of lace edging, this impractical bit of fluff was made to commemorate the Armistice. It's embroidered with the crossed flags of France, the United States, and England who were allies in that war against Germany and the other Central Powers. Under the laurel-leafed entwined flags are the words, "Souvenir de France, 1919." Most likely, such handkerchiefs were quickly manufactured and sold by French shops to American doughboys. Lightweight and portable, they were the perfect gift for the home folks.

Similar embroidered or printed handkerchiefs were also sold to U.S. soldiers and sailors during subsequent wars. Many a mother or sweetheart received a printed handkerchief or a gaudily-embroidered satin pillow after WWII as a memento of some American military overseas involvement.

One of the most unusual handkerchiefs I have ever seen is called a "blood chit." I included such a handkerchief in an exhibit I created in 1994 called *From Vicksburg to Vietnam*. The exhibit represented all wars of United States' involvement during the century between 1860s to the 1960s. A Wacoan named Travis DuBois, brother of Foy DuBois of Eddy, wore a large silk printed handkerchief sewn to the back of his leather flying jacket when he "flew the hump" during WWII. This term described China's treacherously high mountains that U. S. cargo planes had to fly over from India to Burma.

Blood chit was slang for a handkerchief printed in several languages: French, Mandarin, English, and other dialects of that part of the world. (A chit is a voucher that can be exchanged for food, etc.) This handkerchief was a life-saving device for our airmen who flew over that area because China was in a state of complete anarchy. Piratical war lords, who captured a downed American airman, had to be bribed to exchange their captive for ransom. The writing says in each language: "Bring this man in alive and he will be redeemed for cash." Travis DuBois returned as a hero, having flown many dozens of flying missions over China and Europe. He served as Mayor of Waco after his return.

Today, handkerchiefs have lost their popularity, especially for women. Department stores no longer have special sales counters for handkerchiefs. In our throw-away society, the disposable facial tissue is now used by consumers who are too busy to bother with laundering and ironing handkerchiefs. But there was a time when every well-dressed man or woman carried that emblem of refinement, a linen handkerchief or in the case of Flyman Travis DuBois, wore a handkerchief.

Photograph of blood chit handkerchief courtesy of the National Museum of the Pacific War, Fredericksburg, Texas

THE LIFE OF A TEXTILE

Once a textile leaves the loom, it takes many possible forms of life. Fine silk and linen, of course, may be transformed into elegant gowns, upholstery, or window hangings, for instance. They are precious textiles, but folks in the past have always known that all textiles are precious.

Before the modern disposable paper towel, there were many possibilities for a plain piece of simply-loomed cotton. In the Fort House 19th century kitchen, we show several handy, absorbent dish towels. These are emblematic of our grandmothers' recycling efforts, long before the word "recycle" was coined in its modern context. These dish towels—made from flour sacks—began their life spans as sturdy commercial containers, sacks made to hold such kitchen staples as sugar and flour.

The twenty-pound flour sack would have been emptied of its contents into the nearby Hoosier cabinet flour storage bin. The cook would have then carefully wound up the string that sewed the bag closed and set it away for future use, to tie up a roast perhaps. This C and H (which stands for California and Hawaii) Sugar sack has been opened up and used as a dish cloth or dish towel.

Laundered and bleached, it might have been sewn into a sleeping gown or filled with goose down for a bed pillow. I remember that my thrifty Speegleville grandmother used to sew several feed sacks together to make a bed sheet. The coarse fabric grew softer with laundering and wear, but the sleeper still had to contend with those scratchy seams. Some folks considered coarse feed sacks perfect for bath towels.

The housewife had two possibilities: the flour sack made of a tightly woven cotton that usually contained finely ground staples such as flour and sugar and the rustic feed sack that held coarser goods such as oats. The mills quickly realized the commercial possibilities when they saw that housewives favored flour and grains packaged in colorful, printed cotton sacks. Some even began to print borders on their designs, which translated into attractive broomstick skirts. The consumer might buy several sacks packaged in the same color/design , so as to have enough fabric for a man's shirt or matching dresses for two little sisters.

Such precious fabric might have been sewn into baby bibs, potholders, aprons, handkerchiefs, sunbonnets, diapers, or curtains for the kitchen. A square of the fabric could have been made into a bag for straining cream. The tied-up bag filled with cream would have hung from a hook all night, with the curds forming inside the bag and the whey dripping into a container below. The next morning when the bag was opened, a ball of creamy cottage cheese would roll out.

Every woman in the old days had a "ragbag," perhaps a discarded pillowcase, where all excess scraps of textiles would be stored. All the remnants from cutting out a dress would go in, along with worn-out garments, their buttons removed beforehand and stored away in a fruit jar for future use. Then, whenever a piece of fabric was needed for a patch or to replace a worn shirt collar, the solution could always be found in the household ragbag.

Women polished and cleaned stoves and tables; they scoured and scrubbed floors from cellar to attic with feed sack rags. A cloth could be used for dusting furniture or as a sling for a sprained wrist or broken arm. Many of us who were children of the Depression remember our mothers or grandmothers making a play-dress from a couple of flower-sprigged feed sacks. Thus, women expanded flour and feed sack usage beyond their kitchens.

Many women of the 19th century were avid quilters. Some quilts were finely stitched by women of leisure, using carefully selected store-bought fabric and expensive commercial grade cotton batting. For farm women in a hurry, quilts were quickly made with mismatched feed sack fabric and batting from their own cotton field.

There always seemed to be one person in a family who was clever at crocheting rag rugs, which could be made in any size or shape. Cutting rag bag fabric into one-inch wide strips, she would crochet them into handsome, durable rugs that could be used in every room in the house, except perhaps the parlor, which would have demanded something a bit more formal.

The very last place for a textile that had seen its full usage was the rag picker. Every good-size town in the 19th century would have had all sorts of street vendors. Each vendor had a specific cry and the rag picker's was, "Rags to buy! Rags to buy!"

For a few pennies, the rag picker purchased worn out textiles from housewives throughout the neighborhoods. At the end of the day, he would steer his mule-drawn cart to the paper mill where all the day's collection of rags would be sold to be made into paper. Paper was the ultimate exercise in recycling.

So what did women do before there were such modern conveniences as facial tissues and paper towels? With great ingenuity, they recycled every single scrap of fabric for their kitchens, clothing, and dozens of other household uses. They "made do," never discarding anything that could possibly be used in the future. "Waste not, want not" was a way of life for those folks.

THE McCULLOCH QUILT

One of Historic Waco Foundation's prize treasures is displayed in the upstairs bedroom of McCulloch House Museum. It's a 19th century quilt made by the McCulloch ladies, a crazy quilt of many shapes and shades of silk and velvet, per-

sonalized with embroidered signatures of the ladies and their friends who shared in its creation.

What makes this quilt so distinctive is that one of the McCulloch ladies decided that she would create a length of linen lace that would trim the finished quilt's edges. The lace is quite wide, and one edge is crocheted in a saw-tooth design. The soft brown thread was never dyed, so this is flax's true color as it ages.

When I say that she wanted to "create" lace, I mean just that. We know that the lady planted the flax seed in her garden, harvested it in the late spring, and then went through all the arduous labor of processing the flax stalks into spun thread, from which she crocheted the lace. The entire process must have taken many months to complete.

Flax has been significant to mankind since antiquity. I've seen perfectly preserved rolls of Egyptian linen, thousands of years old, in the Metropolitan Museum in New York City. Linen fibers are by their very nature strong and smooth, and the linen spun and woven from them is crisp and easy to clean. While the fiber is being processed for spinning, it resembles long, golden hair. The terms "flaxen locks" and "tow-head" derive from the spinning of flax.

In American Colonial times, the all-powerful English wool industry discouraged the colonists from raising sheep. They were supposed to buy their manufactured woolen goods from England. As a result, almost every farmer turned to flax for a crop. The women of most families spun the flax and then wove their own table and bed linens as well as clothing and other household necessities. With all the time and effort that went into the making of this fine-textured, hardy textile, it's easy to understand why family linens have always been considered so precious.

Miss McCulloch spent months in the long and arduous processing of her flax. The plants were pulled in early July after the blue flowers had been replaced by seed pods. The long stalks were then cured in the sun, after which the pods were removed by ripping or drawing them through an iron comb.

The next step was "retting," whereby the bundles of stalks were soaked in water. Miss McCulloch might have used the creek bed that still exists just behind the house for that purpose. After a few weeks of soaking to soften the fibers, the leaves were removed and the mass was allowed to dry. A "flax-brake," which was made of a double-hinged set of boards on legs resembling a sawhorse, was used to crush and remove the outer, woody material that surrounded the precious interior fibers. They were then tied into bundles and beaten with a pestle until soft and pliable.

The next procedure was "hackling" when the dampened fibers were passed through sets of iron teeth. This removed any remaining short stem pieces, leaving only the long, fine flax fibers. These refined bunches of golden strands were tied in hanks and later arranged on a distaff, which is a long, turned length of wood that attaches vertically to the spinning wheel. The distaff holds the hank of flax, which is to be spun.

A distaff dressed with flax is a thing of beauty, the wheat-colored strands softly criss-crossed with ribbon to hold it all in place. As the spinner pedals the wheel, she pulls flax strands through her fingers, always keeping the tension even, occasionally adjusting the ribbon as the flax is gradually spun out into fine thread. After the spinning process, the

skeins of thread would have been thrown into a bleaching solution of hot water and lye and then spread in the sun for further whitening.

It wasn't until this lengthy process was completed that Miss McCulloch could have begun the actual creation of her lace. Crochet work has always been an important part of a woman's arsenal of the needle arts. Our foremothers were familiar with them all: sewing, quilting, embroidering, tatting, crochet, knitting, and needlepoint.

What a satisfying moment for the lady! Just imagine her pleasure as she arranged herself in her favorite chair, adjusted the light source, and perhaps poured herself a cup of hot tea. With deep relish, she lifted her crochet hook and began to whip off intricate stitchery from the lustrous linen thread that she had so lovingly created from a handful of flax seed.

A QUILT THAT SPEAKS FROM THE PAST

The intrigue of the unknown must have been the deciding factor that day several years ago in a Hillsboro antiques store when, for a mere $30, I purchased a raggedy old cotton quilt for Historic Waco Foundation. At first glance, it was overshadowed by its newer, brighter sister quilts, but I could see there was merit in the finely-stitched fragment of an appliqué quilt, no matter how worn and stained.

Best of all, the maker had embroidered her name, place, and date on the front: "Made by Mrs. Ann Rawls, Coosa County, Alabama, July 25, 1860." Then she had added the name of the pattern: "This is the Pararie Rose." Somehow, that misspelled word made the quilt even more intriguing.

This historic curiosity was stored according to proper museum procedures in a five-foot long, acid-free box in the upstairs storage area of HWF. Safely snuggled

in her bed of acid-free tissue, the Pararie Rose quilt lay asleep like an enchanted princess with her secrets intact.

How does one solve the mystery of such a quilt ending up in Hillsboro, Texas? I had inquired of the clerk about its origins, but she was unable to help except to say that it had come from a local estate sale. Searching through the 1860 United States Census, I discovered that the quilt's creator was the middle-aged wife of a prosperous Southern farmer, William Rawls. They lived in Wetumpka District, which was later cut from Coosa County after the Civil War and is now in Elmore county. I wrote letters to the newspaper in Hillsboro and had correspondence with several people linked to their historic organization. I contacted the Coosa County Historical Society, but no one knew anything about Mrs. Ann Rawls.

Finally, I found through the internet Leah Rawls Adkins of Birmingham, Alabama, the great-great-grandchild of Mrs. Ann Rawls. Delighted to hear of her ancestor's quilt, she told me the story of the descendants of William and Ann Rawls.

The Rawls had eleven children, several of whom moved to Texas. We know that the eldest, John Collier Rawls, born 1829, served throughout the Civil War, moved to Texas afterward and settled in Hillsboro. This quilt quite likely came with John Collier to Texas.

John T. Rawls, born 1832, also moved to Texas; Ann Rawls, born 1838, married Benjamin P. Wooldridge and moved to Texas too. John William Rawls, after escaping from a Yankee prison, walked home and moved to Walker County, Texas. Noah W. Rawls, born 1842, was wounded at the Battle of Lookout Mountain. Afterward, he traveled to Texas in a wagon train, arriving in 1870. Henry C. Rawls, born 1849, settled in Itasca, Texas.

The quilt's red and green appliqué pinwheel design of stylized roses on a white background is repeated in nine large blocks which, when combined, make a regular size square quilt. Mrs. Rawls' affluence can be detected from the makings she chose to create her Pararie Rose.

She had purchased lustrous colored fabric and an expensive grade of commercial batting for this project that would have been more expensive than using various scraps from her ragbag and locally grown cotton for batting. The exceedingly fine stitches might indicate this particular project was to be her masterpiece, proudly signed and dated.

Today, l50 years later, the Pararie Rose is a faded reminder of its former pristine self. All four edges have been worn away, and there are some stains and several burn marks. Someone has obviously given it a lot of rough usage over the years.

Then in l996, the local Homespun Quilters' Guild helped document the entire collection of thirty-five HWF quilts. Kathleen McCrady, a well-known quilt expert, came from Austin to carefully analyze, research, and evaluate each quilt.

All guild members pitched in to help. We pulled out all the quilts from storage and arranged them in order of their catalog numbers. We set up a vertical frame from which to pin each open quilt while it was carefully photographed in detail, back and front. I created a form that could be filled out with the pertinent data of each piece and appointed McGrady a secretary to do this job. Details of each quilt were recorded, such as type of fabric, batting, name, value, and date of the quilt design.

When the Pararie Rose was presented to McGrady, she exclaimed, "What have we here? This appliqué pattern is unique to my experience. As damaged and worn as it is, this is a very precious historic piece because it's signed." She explained that few women of the past thought to identify their work.

Guild president, Ellis Bennett, decided to undertake the daunting task of creating a graphed pattern from the Pararie Rose. She spent an entire summer on this project, and HWF now sells the Pararie Rose pattern with all its instructions.

This enthusiasm carried over into the creation of two new Pararie Rose quilts from Ellis Bennett's pattern. All the members of the guild worked on appliqué blocks, spending a total of 500 hours on the project. One replica quilt was generously given to the Heritage Collection of Historic Waco Foundation and the other was raffled off at the Waco quilt show as a fundraiser for the Homespun Quilters' Guild.

Through the industry of the ladies of the Homespun Quilters' Guild, the entire quilt collection of HWF's Heritage Collection now has a large three-ringed notebook filled with all documentation and photographs of every piece, including the Pararie Rose as well as the beautiful crisp, new replica that rests alongside the original.

A STITCH IN TIME SAVES NINE

Close examination of Historic Waco Foundation's four Victorian house museums reveals an inventory of more than a dozen sewing-related artifacts. Sewing machines, sewing chairs, sewing tables, dressmaker dummies, sewing kits, and baskets all testify to the great popularity of needlework in times gone by.

For women who ran households, whether modest or grand, a talent for sewing was a necessity. A husband might need a shirt collar turned or the children might need new school clothes. The Victorian house was filled with textile furnishings that demanded constant upkeep and repair, such as bed linen, curtains, and table linen.

A thrifty housewife saved all her leftover sewing scraps in the ever-present ragbag. She never knew when she might need a bit of fabric to concoct a patch, piece a quilt, or braid a rag rug. As worn-out garments were designated to the ragbag, all buttons would have been removed and stored away for later use. Buttons were always a precious commodity in those days and they were never thrown away. I remember my Waco grandmother always kept her buttons in a big fruit jar. When I was very little, she would give me a needle on a long string and I would spend hours sorting and stringing buttons of all sizes and colors.

The most important technological breakthrough for sewing since the invention of the needle (hand sewing goes back 20,000 years) was the treadle sewing machine.

American Elias Howe is usually credited with its invention. Actually, there were several 18th century European inventors who dabbled with the idea of such a machine. It took a true entrepreneur such as Isaac Merritt Singer to improve upon Howe's idea to produce a chain of continuous stitching. He opportunistically slapped his name on the machine, ultimately making more than

twenty improvements and a fortune in the bargain. Singer's product first came on the market in 1851.

Can you imagine the impact such a machine would have made on a 19th century household? The output and income of a seamstress would have quadrupled. Just think of all those voluminous skirts of Victorian times with dozens of long seams. Suddenly, a seamstress could buzz through that mind-numbing task with great speed. In big cities such as New York, shirt factories produced great quantities of garments from this new technology.

The visitor can see a good example of a treadle sewing machine at East Terrace House Museum in the cupola room. Dated 1860, it is finished in handsome walnut veneer with a detachable lid. The label reads "Willcox & Gibbs Sewing Machine Co., New York, London, Paris." It was given to HWF by Miss Cora Lee Hatch of Lorena.

At Earle-Napier-Kinnard House Museum, we show an alternative to the treadle, the hand-cranked model, which is lightweight and quite portable. This dainty little mechanism is made of cast iron, 1880, and was given to HWF by Mr. & Mrs. Jo Allen Spears. It is labeled "Meader & Co., Cincinnati, Ohio."

I remember that my country grandmother used her old treadle well into the 1930s, since remote Texas farms weren't strung with electrical lines until late in that decade. Even into the 1940s when I was taking sewing classes at West Junior High School on 15th Street, our equipment was a bank of old treadle sewing machines. They were antiquated, but adequate and easy to operate. Today, old treadles are being rounded up and shipped off to Third World countries. They are a natural for such electricity-deprived places. My grandmother's Singer treadle stands in my guest room, in perfect shape and ready to run up a seam or two.

The first electrified sewing machine in Waco now stands in the servant's bedroom at McCulloch House Museum. It was returned to Historic Waco Foundation by a woman in Fredonia, N.Y., Ione Drake-Reiss in 1995, who made this claim about its provenance.

And then there were luxury sewing items such as the 1880 sewing table of black paper maché in East Terrace House Museum's front parlor. Given to HWF by the W.W. Callan Estate, this elegant sewing table has been decorated with tinted mother-of-pearl inlay. Unlock it and the interior is all fitted with tiny spools of thread, needles, and other sewing accoutrements.

Another sewing stand at Earle-Napier-Kinnard House Museum is of oak with a turned pedestal tripod base, circa 1880. This was a gift of the late Joanne McCulley, a member of that house for many years. It stands on the upstairs' landing, an appropriate location since many ladies preferred to work upstairs out of the way of household traffic and noise.

Earle-Napier-Kinnard House Museum has another sewing table, 1880, standing on tripod French scroll feet, rounded burled top with octagonal space compartments. Donated by Frances Duncan Nalle, it is located in the south bedroom. Also at Kinnard is a sewing machine table of walnut with a lyre-base, 1870. At East Terrace House Museum in the Mann's bedroom is a walnut sewing table of Eastlake style with a beveled top and burled veneer splayed legs. Its wooden casters, which gave the furniture mobility, are quite typical of Victorian times.

One of my favorite sewing pieces is the sewing cabinet at Fort House Museum, donated by E.C. Bolton. It's in the form of a small 3-drawer chest with extensions on either side. The sides bulge out like the panniers on an 18th century dress. Its top raises up to reveal storage space inside for spools of thread, needles, and scissors. These sewing tables were very popular in the 19th century and were known as Martha Washington style. Located in the same bedroom is a small, folding sewing chair of gumwood, circa 1860. It formerly stood in the William Abeel castle on Austin Avenue and was donated to HWF by Mrs. Maurice Barnes.

Marquetry top of 1880 sewing table.

Today, fewer and fewer women choose to sew at home. Those leisurely days, when a housewife sewed for her family and passed the skills down to her daughters, are long gone. Today's fast-running commercial sewing machines zip up over 2,000 stitches a minute.

TOILE DE JOUY

About fifteen years ago on a visit to Paris, I took the train to the town of Versailles, and then a cab to the Musée de la Toile de Jouy. Housed in a small 18th century château, the museum exhibits the equipment, textiles, costumes, and bed hangings that tell the story of Toile de Jouy.

I was greeted by the conservator, Madame Guillaume, who gave me a tour of the facility. She graciously unlocked glass cases so I could photograph the displays more easily. I spent the entire day there, studying the lovely original toiles that once entranced the likes of Queen Marie Antoinette and Empress Joséphine. I was shown two beautiful 18th century beds with all their elaborate toile hangings that had just been purchased at auction. I was amazed at their crisp, unfaded condition.

Toile, in French, means linen or cotton, and de Jouy denotes the small town where these cottons were printed. Sometime during the mid-18th century, a German printer named Christophe-Philippe Oberkampf, 1738-1815, took up residence near the little town of Jouy-en-Josas, which is in the vicinity of the Palace of Versailles. Oberkampf built a factory nearby and began to turn out beautiful textiles. Originally, the toiles were hand-printed with wooden blocks. Copper plates were an improvement in quality, but then Oberkampf devised etched copper rollers that greatly increased production.

One of his most easily recognized designs incorporated images of peasants amidst their fields, with ancient ruins nearby, printed in a single color on white cotton. Soon, Oberkampf would glean design ideas from all that was currently happening in France: court life, celebrities, battle scenes, politics, and both the American and French revolutions. More than thirty thousand different patterns would emanate from the factory there at the town of Jouy, which is next to the river Josas.

Originally, toiles were monochromatic, a single color (red, blue, black, or a deep shade of violet) on the natural white background. Soon, toiles became more complex with added colors in the designs. All dyes were derived from natural sources.

Patterns were drawn by a staff of talented artists. One imaginative and very popular design idea was the American Revolution, which featured Benjamin Franklin, a popular hero among the French. Napoléon Bonaparte's 1799 Egyptian campaign was commemorated with a fanciful design of camels, pyramids, palm trees, sphinxes, and obelisks. This particular design is currently being reproduced in black on white by Clarence House.

As dictated by the state, every thirty foot-length of Oberkampf toile was stamped with the government-mandated manufacturer's guarantee. There may have been other printers who attempted to duplicate his ideas, but Oberkampf's high-quality printed designs were the ones that knowledgeable, stylish people coveted.

Of all the visitors to Oberkampf's factory, the most astounding must have been Emperor Napoléon and Empress Joséphine in 1806. The Empress was a talented decorator and had used Oberkampf's toiles in several of her design projects. That day, the Emperor presented Oberkampf with the coveted Legion of Honor, a decoration that Napoléon had created in 1802.

Toiles de Jouy were immensely successful. Oberkampf had chosen his site well, locating his factory near the Palace of Versailles. Passing noblemen took note and began to visit the factory and to order the beautiful textiles. It soon became fashionable to decorate an entire room in a single design: walls, bed hangings, and upholstered furniture.

Though the factory closed in 1843, toiles have never lost their appeal. Indeed, toile de Jouy is a classic. Like the Egyptian tribute toile of Napoléon's invasion of Egypt, several of the original designs are still printed. In the museum in France, there is a remnant of cotton serge with a block print of tiger-skin design, circa 1806, which was once used to decorate a billiard room. Today, we think of leopard or tiger-skin design as be-

Toile-backed quilt,
Earle-Napier-Kinnard House Museum

ing very new and trendy. Not necessarily, it was extremely popular in the first part of the 19th century there in France.

Toile, from the very beginning, has been a perfect medium for printing the latest news. The idea of a political message being sent to the public via a toile design was implemented as early in France as 1820 when their abolition movement became active. Later in the 1860s, the United States abolition movement also saw the beauty in such an idea.

Printed in violet on white background is a scene of African natives being kidnapped by slave dealers. It is titled *Traite des Negres*, ie. Slave Trade. This rare historic textile, printed about 1835-40 in Rouen, France, was recently exhibited at Winterthur Museum in Delaware and they have generously shared this image with us.

Credit: Courtesy, Winterthur Museum, textile, Traite des Negres, museum purchase, 2002.36

Here in late 19th century Waco, toile was seldom used. The only trace of a toile in our Historic Waco Foundation houses is a red on white design on the back of a lovely old quilt displayed at Earle-Napier-Kinnard House Museum. I have chosen to use this particular toile design for the cover of my book.

THE ORIGINS OF
HISTORIC WACO FOUNDATION

Generous intentions are useless unless one level-headed leader steps up to coordinate a project. **Shepherd Spencer Neville Brown, Sr.** (1920-2009) was just that sort of man, many times over. This significant Wacoan is no longer with

us, and our city will miss his influence and many generous gestures. One project that he coordinated is our own Historic Waco Foundation, which grew from the original donations of several patrons. Since this story concerns Spencer Brown and the origins of Historic Waco Foundation, it is worth relating to my readers. After I completed this account, I asked Tom Collins—a long- time member of the Waco Foundation Board of Directors—to check it for accuracy. He gave his approval and declared that the following is factual.

In 1958, Robert B. Parrott and his wife, Edith Heinze Parrott, who lived in Indianapolis, initiated the idea of establishing the Waco Perpetual Growth Foundation. The couple, who had roots in Waco, donated $30,000 as seed money to start this community fund to benefit the city. Hoping to inspire Wacoans at-large to contribute, the couple promised to match any gifts up to a rather large amount over several years. Time went by with little matching funds coming in, and the time limit was just about to expire.

Meanwhile, the William A. Fort House had been purchased by the Junior League and given to Waco Perpetual Growth Foundation (subsequently changed to Historic Waco Foundation.) In 1960, F. M. Young of Young Brothers Construction Company of Waco and owner of East Terrace donated this valuable historic property to The Heritage Society of Waco. Each house had its support group and they had made some renovations; however, upkeep funds were scarce.

At one point, $6,000 was needed to complete the renovation of Fort House. Spencer Brown's father, Stanton Brown, phoned all his friends and collected the needed money. Some of the first benefactors of Historic Waco Foundation were:

Stanton Brown, Roger Conger, Harlon Fentress, V.M. Cox, Howard Hambleton, Harry Provence, J.H. Kultgen, John Murchison, Walter Lacy, Jr., W.W. Naman, and W.R. Phillips. These names are recorded on a bronze plaque, which hangs in the entrance hall of Fort House.

Knowing that he was a banker and an influential community leader, a concerned group then asked Spencer Brown if he could help with matching the Parrott offer. This was in the early 1970s. From a surviving letter, Spencer Brown tells the story of the creation of the Historic Waco Foundation and the Waco Foundation: "The Boards were doing a great job with what little funds they had. Mrs. Baker Duncan Nalle had personally bought the Earle-Napier-Kinnard House and was trying to keep it up as an historical house from her home in Austin."

"I came up with the idea of contributing the value of all three houses to match the Parrott Fund. The real challenge was to talk Mrs. Nalle into giving up her house. After several sessions with her, I was able to explain that the Parrott Fund would match all of the values of three homes and their antique contents. This would mean that all three houses would have some operating funds from this income."

"My greatest accomplishment was to get Mrs. Nalle to give all her Duncan Foundation, as well as the Earle-Napier-Kinnard house, if the two other historic homes were also given. The gift value of these historic homes and the Duncan Foundation were matched by Robert Parrott and the Historic Waco Foundation was born."

Historic Waco Foundation was formed in 1967 through the merger and incorporation of three common interest groups: the Heritage Society, the Society for Historic Preservation and the Duncan Foundation. Founders of the original combined organization included Roger N. Conger, Harlon M. Fentress, and Sally Carlisle.

From these early beginnings of the Historic Waco Foundation and The Waco Foundation, the founders began a fundraiser called "The Pilgrimage" in the early 1960s, which occurred in the springtime. Mrs. Barclay (Margaret) Megarity headed up The Pilgrimage fundraiser, and Mrs. Maurice (Bobbie) Barnes directed the furnishing of the houses.

By then, McCulloch House (badly damaged by the '53 tornado) had been given to HWF by the McCulloch heirs and brought into the fold. All participants of The Pilgrimage dressed in Old Southern-style costumes and the four houses were open for visitation. The Pilgrimage lasted for three or four years and could be considered the forerunner of what later became the Brazos River Festival and is associated with the modern revival of the Cotton Palace Pageant.

Spencer Brown went on to chair fundraising campaigns for Providence Hospital, United Way, Vanguard School Board of Trustees, Downtown Rotary Club, and St. Paul's Episcopal Day School. He also served as a director and executive committee member of King's Daughters' Hospital Board of Trustees (Temple,) Woodberry Forest Board of Trustees (Virginia,) Baylor Alumni Association, Waco Library Association, and the Railroad Museum (Temple.)s Spencer Brown served as president of Hedonia Club of Waco. He was a key founder of Vanguard School and numerous other community organizations that still thrive today, including Historic Waco Foundation. In 1977, he was honored as King of the Waco Cotton Palace Pageant and by Vanguard High School, whose main building carries his name today.

Spencer Brown was a credit to his community. As his son, Stanton Boyce Brown, explained in his father's April 14, 2009 Waco Tribune-Herald obituary, "So many of his contributions to Waco have been made quietly and/or anonymously. The above instance of his influence with Historic Waco Foundation is only one of many, too numerous to enumerate."

ABOUT THE AUTHOR

Though born in Dallas, Texas, I've always considered Waco my hometown. I grew up here, attending local schools and graduating from Waco High School on Columbus Avenue. Waco had been home to my great-grandparents, Emma Eliza Hooper and Lyman Gould Armstrong, who came to Texas from Alabama after the Civil War.

Their daughter was Mrs. Alda Sanderson of Speegleville, whose home was near the edge of old Lake Waco. I spent many a pleasant summer visiting my grandmother, learning to appreciate the harmony of farm life with all its animals, hard work, and slow-paced days.

As a young woman, I traveled a great deal and lived in several of this country's great metropolitan areas: Los Angeles, New York, and San Francisco. It was there that I met my future husband, Peter Masters, and we settled in a small community across the bay from San Francisco to rear our daughter, Alda.

I began to write freelance for several Bay Area newspapers, developing a shopper column that gained a certain popularity with my readers. Over twenty years, more than 500 articles appeared under my by-line on subjects as far-ranging as family health, art history, gardening, fashion, food, interior décor, architecture, book reviews, travel, and art and theater criticism. Fashion history, in particular, was a favorite because I had begun a lifelong project to study, lecture, collect, and travel in order to expand my knowledge on the subject.

Retiring about thirty years ago, my husband and I sought a slower-paced life and we happily retired to Waco where I still had family and childhood friends. My re-introduction to Waco was the day I produced an antique hat fashion show to benefit Waco Garden Clubs, and that's how I first met Bobbie Barnes, and she invited me to help with the HWF clothing collections.

I was to spend the next twenty years sorting, cataloging, and creating twenty-eight exhibits, which displayed many of those historic garments. I gave the clothing collection its name, The Heritage Collection. This treasure trove of local history now consists of approximately 3,000 garments and flat textiles, which are currently stored at HWF's office, Hoffmann House.

Bobbie Barnes is gone now. With her all-abiding interest in the decorative arts, she set the pace for all of us at Historic Waco Foundation and I have tried to keep the faith. Over the last ten years, I have written 120 *Portals to the Past* columns. This book shares some of the most successful of those columns.

CLAIRE ARMSTRONG MASTERS

(Left) The author on her wedding day to Peter Masters, 1963. Mark Hopkins Hotel, San Francisco.

(Below) Jacob Peter Smith, the author's grandson, 2011.

Peter and Claire had one daughter, Alda, who is the old-fashioned girl on page 80. Alda has just given them a grandson, Jacob Peter Smith, who will celebrate his first birthday this September.

ACKNOWLEDGMENTS

I wish to thank Carlos Sanchez, former Editor of *Waco Tribune-Herald*, for granting permission to reprint these stories of mine, which were originally seen in *Waco Today* magazine. My gratitude to Watson Arnold, President of Historic Waco Foundation, for his encouragement of this project. Also, many thanks to my daughter, Alda Masters-Smith, and Claude Valahu, who proofread this book, and to my husband, Peter, who offered helpful suggestions. Thank you to Don Edwards and José Yau, who photographed all these beautiful illustrations. Another thank you to John Chatmas, McLennan Community College instructor, who helped with architectural imagery. Kudos to Kim Williams of By Design, who with her infinite patience, is responsible for the "look" of this publication, and to Allen Chick of Davis Brothers Publishing Company, who patiently walked me through the labyrinth of its production. Despite his sight-impairment, my dear friend Don Oliver lent his expertise in the final reading of my book. Many thanks to others who gave their time and expertise when I was originally researching and writing these articles.

THE AUTHOR

All proceeds from the sale of this book benefit Historic Waco Foundation

LAGNIAPPE
"a little something extra"

I wonder what their stories were....?

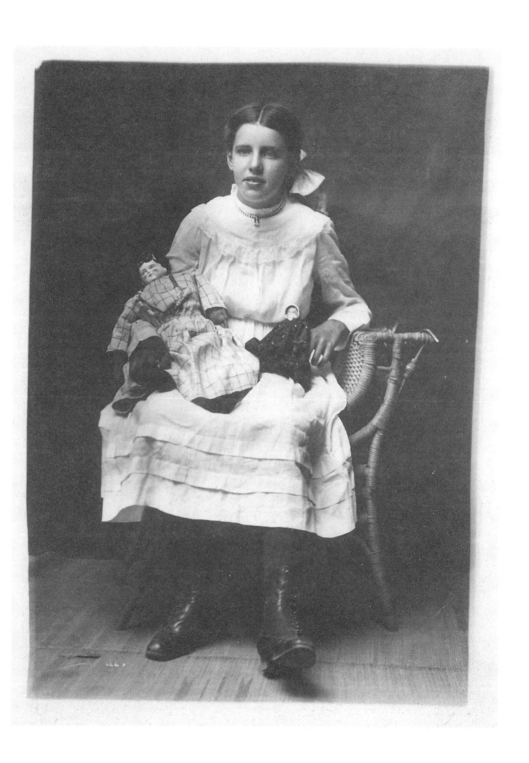

176

Off to the Dog & Pony Show
at Giddings Tex. Oct. 20, 1903.

(Above) Eb Morrow and his twin brother, Calvin.

Decatur, Ill., U. S. A.
Home Office and Factory.

1048. "Just like mamma does."
Cor't'd. 1902. by C. L. Wasson.